SCHOOLCRAFT COLLEGE LIBRARY

W9-BRQ-291

E
840.8
.M85
A34

Muskie,
Journeys

WITHDRAWN

JOURNEYS

———

JOURNEYS

Edmund S. Muskie

Doubleday & Company, Inc.   Garden City, New York

1972

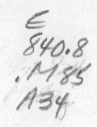

E
840.8
.M85
A34

Library of Congress Catalog Card Number 71-190432
Copyright © 1972 by Edmund S. Muskie
All Rights Reserved
Printed in the United States of America
First Edition

CONTENTS

To my father and mother, Jane, and the kids

ACKNOWLEDGMENTS

This book reflects the influence of my father and mother and my life with Jane and our children. And it would not be possible if it were not for the countless contributions of thousands of friends who have given me inspiration and help over the years.

My immediate thanks go to Samuel S. Vaughan and Donald E. Nicoll, who edited the material for the book from the outpourings of a sometimes long-winded senator, and to Miss Lorelei J. Williams and Miss Elsie N. Vance who typed the manuscript and checked the facts.

Edmund S. Muskie
Washington, D.C.
March 1972

JOURNEYS

———

Preface

ONCE, at the close of a meeting with President-elect Nixon and Vice-President Humphrey after the 1968 campaign, I was asked by the press to make a comment. It seemed to me that everyone else had said what there was to say and so I answered with an old saying from Maine: When you have nothing to say, don't try to improve on silence.

I don't know whether this little book will be an improvement on silence, but at the time it is being written, there is some curiosity about who I am, where I'm from, and what I am for. It is unlikely that all such questions can be satisfactorily answered here. Some can best be answered by others. Individual issues, such as the environment, require a whole book. I have tried instead to put down a few reflections on who I am, what I am, where I came from, and what I would like our country to be.

This is not a book of staff-produced "position papers."
Nor is it a full-scale autobiography, which would be pre-
sumptuous and—I like to think—premature. It is a series
of notes on experiences and ideals, recollections, opinions,
and recommendations.

The reader will have to decide whether silence might
have been preferable.

Despite all that, JOURNEYS becomes, inevitably, I suppose,
a "campaign book." The usual practice is for a candidate
to have a book (or books) written about him, full of
praise, with copies widely circulated and widely unread
among the party faithful—and pressed into the hands of
those who have not yet pledged allegiance. A book or two
has been written about me, as well as yards of journalism,
and some of what has been written is not wide of the
mark. Still, I do think that a man ought to, when he can,
speak for himself.

So, for better or worse, this is my campaign book. By
the time it appears, I may be the Democratic nominee for
President or out of contention. What I have tried to do is
not just to keep my candidacy in mind but to make the
book useful to journalists and historians, as well as to my
wife and children and to our grandchildren—that is, of some
value beyond 1972.

Perhaps it will help to answer some of the questions that
have swirled around my head and heels since the time when
I, for many people at least, surfaced during the national
political convention and campaign of 1968.

The book is meant to be my view of unfinished journeys.
I refer especially to the journeys of my father and of millions
like him, who came to this country with a vision of a
greater nation than mankind had ever known. JOURNEYS is
also a commentary on our unfinished voyage toward that

vision, as well as toward the promise of freedom and equality that is the only justification for a democratic society. And because the writing is personal, it is inescapably the story of my own unfinished journey to wherever I am going.

The outline of my family's life is familiar to some and not very startling. But the meaning is important to me and the place of such stories in our history counts for something. My life is less important than what it represents—the fact that in spite of our troubles and shortcomings, the United States is a place to come to, to be born in, to grow in, and to love. It has been so for my family and I want to help to make it so for each member of our society, particularly for those who have not been so lucky as I.

CHAPTER I

●

The Roads to 1968

LATE IN THE evening on March 31, 1968, my wife and I were in the living room of our home in Washington. We settled down to listen to a speech by the President. I thought the speech was very impressive. I was delighted at the decision to halt most of the bombing of North Vietnam. Although we didn't know quantitatively how much of a halt there would be, it was obviously a major decision and I was pleased for the sake of the countries involved and at the improved prospect for peace. The political implications were favorable, too, and I was not immune to those. Then, when President Johnson slipped into the last sentences of his address, I wasn't sure that I understood what we were hearing. It was a different subject, it seemed out of context, and I was virtually numb when he finished.

I shared with the rest of the country the profound shock and surprise that Lyndon Johnson had taken himself out of the race. Whatever the official starting dates, the campaign of 1968 began for me, as it did for most other people, at that instant.

Senator Eugene McCarthy had announced earlier, but not everyone took his announcement seriously. Those of us who knew him realized that he was deeply motivated by his convictions to do something, but we were not certain where those convictions would lead him. I admired his courage, but like many other people I wasn't sure of the political significance of his candidacy.

At the outset, I did not think that Gene had much of a chance. Even at the beginning of the New Hampshire primary campaign, the prospects for his candidacy did not seem overly promising. I did not participate in that campaign, but I did get a reading on the impact of his candidacy when I went home to Maine and inquired about how Gene was doing in New Hampshire. Maine observers felt he wasn't making headway up to that point.

This was not an exhaustive political poll. I just asked friends who knew something about the New Hampshire situation. We did learn that the activities in behalf of President Johnson were running into trouble. His name was not even on the ballot and it would have to be a write-in campaign, in which many voters could simply forget to write in his name. Gene was on the ballot and the name of Lyndon Johnson was not, and such simple facts have a considerable importance, although such "details" tend to be forgotten with the passage of time. The Johnson people were at work, but my impression was that they weren't as effective as they could have been. The regular state party

organization was working for the President. The McCarthy
people were young men and women coming in from outside, plus the anti-war activists within the state, and they
weren't well organized at first. Nevertheless, the pros did
not appear to be handling their public relations very effectively. In any case it was assumed when I checked that
the President would have no difficulty and that McCarthy
was getting nowhere. So much for checking the grass roots
by looking at the other fellow's yard.

Before his decision, I wrote the President two letters, one
on the war in Vietnam, and another evaluating the political
situation. In one, I said that in my judgment the people
wanted to get out of Vietnam. The polls seemed to divide
people into hawks and doves, but they fell into these
categories only because they differed on how best to get out.
It was not so much a question of whether we went for
a military victory or whether we surrendered. That wasn't
the point. I wanted him to understand clearly that in my
judgment most folks simply wanted out. I said that I would
be amazed if the results in New Hampshire did not reflect
this sentiment. I was not predicting the ultimate vote for
Gene McCarthy because it was still my impression that he
wasn't doing much politically.

My opinion about the war was not a matter of polls,
either. Nor was it a question of soliciting opinions. It was
people stopping me on the street and bringing up the subject of the war. Why are we there? What sense does this
make? Why aren't we getting out? It was grass roots, very
pervasive. I sensed it, saw it everywhere. It was not just
young people; it was people of all ages, and especially in
my home town of Waterville, where I had known people
for a quarter of a century or more. There they feel personally
as well as politically related to me and they were going out

of their way to talk about the war—something that people don't do very often on a political issue. They don't get excited about issues and stop you on the street to urge a course of action—at least not often in my part of the country.

The reaction to the war was so strong, I thought the President should know it, and I wasn't sure that he was getting this kind of information from his regular sources.

Before I wrote him about politics, I wrote him about the war. I told him I thought that stopping the bombing could be an important initiative to take, and I suggested that we risk it in unilateral form; it might work. That suggestion was not based on military advice because there was no easy way for me to get it at that time. It was a political opinion, a diplomatic opinion, and a humane opinion. I was not writing as a potential candidate. The President, we assumed, was going to seek re-election. No one had much doubt about that despite the fact that Gene McCarthy had entered the race and there was widespread dissatisfaction about the war and its effect on the country. My letter was an attempt to influence the policies of an administration I assumed would continue in office. I don't know whether that letter had any influence. To this day I don't know how he reacted to that letter, if at all.

Lyndon Johnson was, perhaps, never happy about what I wrote to him. In 1965, Senators Mike Mansfield, George Aiken, Hale Boggs, Daniel Inouye, and I went to Vietnam and to other countries at the President's request. When we came back we set down our findings. Later, President Johnson said this to me about the results of the Mansfield mission: "I didn't have to send you fellows halfway around the world to learn what you said in that report."

Then he added: "I already knew it."

That presents an interesting question, because we had

written in the report a prediction that we were involved
in an open-ended war. If, in fact, he shared this view, if
he already knew it and had the same disquiet we expressed,
then this would raise more troublesome questions about his
policies in Vietnam at that time. In any case, he was not
happy with our report in 1965, and he was probably not
happy with my letters in January and February 1968.

My relations with Lyndon Johnson have fluctuated widely.
I know he admired some of my work, and he depended
heavily on me from time to time, but he did not always
think that I did everything well, or that I treated him as
I should, particularly when I first appeared as a freshman
senator and went to pay a courtesy call on the Majority
Leader.

Lyndon Johnson then, as later, was a big man: in body,
in vision, and in ambition. He talked to me for a while
about the difficulty of adjusting as a new senator, especially
as a senator who had been a governor. He said that the
tough times were when you had to vote, when you went on
record.

"Many times, Ed," he said, "you won't know how you're
going to vote until the clerk who's calling the roll gets to
the M's."

This made sense to me and I appreciated the advice. He
was my leader and I needed advice.

Senator Johnson then turned to the legislative program
for the coming session. He took great pains to explain to
me—and I will admit to feeling some pressure—that there
was a vote coming up on the filibuster. Lyndon wanted me
to vote with his compromise measure, one that would call
for the end of a debate when voted by two thirds of the
members present in the Senate. I thought that another plan,

a compromise that called for a three-fifths vote, was probably preferable, but I wasn't, at that moment, entirely sure. When he had finished explaining and, in effect, giving me some rather strong guidelines on how to vote, he remarked: "Well, Ed, you don't seem to have much to say."

"Lyndon," I answered, "the clerk hasn't gotten to the M's yet."

I was not trying to be rude or impertinent, but I suppose he took it that way. I just wanted him to know I wasn't quite ready to buy and that I had not committed myself to any other proposal, either. I was reserving judgment. When I decided, I voted against the Majority Leader and for the "liberal" plan.

The committee assignments I drew as a new senator were not considered to be exactly plums. I was kept off the committees which I had indicated as my first choices: Foreign Relations, Interstate and Foreign Commerce, and Judiciary. Banking and Currency was one I had indicated an interest in—it was my fourth choice—and I was so assigned, but the other two committees, Public Works and Government Operations, were not a major interest at that time.

In the long run, perhaps it was just as well. Such committees gave me the chance to work on problems of increasing importance to the country. In fact, the combination of Banking and Currency, Government Operations, and Public Works was unique in the Senate, and working in and between those committees I was caught up in most of the legislative efforts to improve the quality of urban life in America. Senator Johnson had done me a favor, although I don't think he had planned it that way.

The Senate has been described as a "club," and with some reason. But it isn't really a club in the sense that most of us think of social or fraternal organizations. It's not even

a truly deliberative body. Before going to the Senate, I had
the notion that members would meet on a continuing basis
and discuss profound questions of public policy, debating in
public or over lunch or perhaps over a drink in the afternoon. It turned out to be not that kind of place at all.
You don't see the other senators very often and you rarely
get a chance to discuss many serious issues with them.
We are all too busy. We are a group of one hundred individuals, each tied down to his office work and his committee work. Committee work is so extensive now that you
rarely have more than one or two senators sitting with you
during the hearings. Days can go by when you don't run
into more than one or two senators.

To be sure, there are occasional extended debates on the
floor, but the old picture of the Senate as a forum that may
have been true for the nineteenth century, or even the early
twentieth, certainly isn't true today. There are even fewer
extensive debates today than in, say, Lyndon Johnson's time
as Majority Leader.

If I have any criticism of the Senate as an institution, it
relates to the absence of consistent pressure. Authority and
focus are diffuse, and individual members tend to find their
own way, without the pressures of party discipline inherent
in a parliamentary system or, at least during the Nixon
administration, the challenge of persistent leadership from
the White House. It is pressure that makes anyone grow, a
stimulating climate, and that is as true of political life as
of any other life, whether it is plant or animal life or
human beings.

In the Senate you could get by with a minimum of effort and pressure, I suppose. I can't think of any senator who
would try to loaf his way through this institution, but I
can see where it might be possible. Your time is your own

and there are no clock watchers. If you didn't want to turn out any legislation at all you could operate that way, and some voters might think that was a good idea.

More substantially, however, there is no workable way at the moment for the Senate to lay out a program for this country. Individual senators introduce legislation, and we consider legislation which the President initiates, but the Senate has no way of acting collectively except in response to initiatives by individuals that are unrelated to any over-all Senate plan. As Majority Leader, Lyndon Johnson used a sort of State of the Union message of his own to focus on legislation he thought was necessary. That was a road map for the Democratic side of the Senate. But by and large the Senate does not have a plan, even though individual senators have a considerable creative capacity for generating ideas that find their way into the law, at times wisely, at times otherwise.

The textbook image of the Senate in session is not really accurate, and neither is the image of the cloakroom—the place where deals are made. To be literal, first, the cloakroom is not a very active place these days because senators don't even go to the floor very often or for very long. The cloakroom is, nevertheless, symbolic of a process that is inevitable in legislation. That is the horse trading and the dealing and swapping, the honest compromise, which is, by and large, a legitimate process. But most of the swapping of ideas and compromising take place in committees, where legislation is put together. We have to do it between the two Houses when the House and the Senate disagree, meeting in conference to work out disagreements. The legislative process *is* compromise and without it you can't get anywhere. To work compromises without destroying the integrity of legislation is an art.

Despite my criticism of the process, the quality of the new senators coming along is pretty high. I know those on my side of the aisle better than I do those on the Republican side but I think that over-all there is a new breed of senator—serious minded, less partisan in a sense, although some can be partisan enough, and younger. The average age of senators has dropped considerably in the last ten years. This trend might have been started by Jack Kennedy's ascension to the presidency and the whole emphasis on youth which followed in the '60s. Television contributes, too, by taking control of candidacies away from the party organizations. Whatever it defects, television has had this liberating effect. It has also led to more challenges to traditional arrangements within the Senate. Seniority and customs of deference are being chipped away by men and women who use television and other media to influence congressional institutions from the outside.

My own legislative career reflects some of the changes that have taken place in the Senate. The Legislative Reorganization Act of 1946 had reduced the number of standing committees and had spelled out the jurisdiction of the several committees, but that framework wasn't adequate for changing circumstances or senatorial ambitions. By the end of the 1950s, when I entered the Senate, the members had developed the creation of new subcommittees to a fine art. To the cynical it was another example of political aggrandizement, and the cynics were partly right. One of the less attractive sides of the subcommittee build-up has been the occasional clash between subcommittee and committee chairmen over legislative jurisdiction. That has been a small price, however, for the contributions legislative subcommittees have made to the development of national policies. As a matter of fact, the competition between subcommittees has provided one of the few pressure points in the Senate, and, as I have noted before, I think the Senate needs more constant pressure.

My first subcommittee was the Government Operations Subcommittee on Intergovernmental Relations. The title is enough to put most reporters and readers to sleep, but the work of the subcommittee has made possible some exciting changes in the way government deals with individual citizens. As a governor, I had been troubled by the way federal programs got locked into patterns that no longer served their original purposes. Sometimes they outlived the original need. As the governor of a relatively poor state I wasn't about to campaign for an end to federal aid, and as a politician concerned with the protection of individual rights and equal opportunity I had no intention of calling for the return of all powers to the states. I knew too much about the short-comings and the inequities of state and local governments. But I did believe that federal grants in aid could be loosened up, and I was convinced that we needed more flexibility for state and local governments to experiment with new approaches to old, intractable problems like housing and community redevelopment, poverty and unemployment, law enforcement and corrections, planning and environmental protection, education and health services. I didn't think that all wisdom flowed from Washington, and I was convinced that more flexible and creative relationships could be developed between federal, state, and local governments.

One of my first initiatives as a senator was to sponsor legislation creating the Advisory Commission on Intergovernmental Relations, an advisory body of federal, state, and local officials who would have a continuing responsibility for making studies and recommendations to improve the federal system. The legislation was enacted and subcommittees were set up in the Senate and the House of Representatives to monitor the work of the Commission. I became chairman of the Senate subcommittee as well as a member of the Commission.

The subcommittee developed a number of useful proposals over the years, none of which got much public attention. Two in particular have a great potential in making government more responsive and responsible. The first is the Uniform Relocation Assistance Act. The second is the Metropolitan Development Act, which became Title II of the Demonstration Cities and Metropolitan Development Act, more popularly known as the Model Cities Act. As a governor I had encountered the problems of homeowners and small businessmen whose land was taken under federal highway programs. In too many cases they had no place to go to re-create the home they had known or the business they had operated profitably. The compensation for their property was inadequate, and they almost never got enough money for moving expenses and those intangible costs associated with relocation. What compensation and relocation assistance programs existed seemed more attuned to keeping the land-taking costs low than to making good those most injured in the process. I soon discovered in hearings before the Banking and Currency Committee, which has jurisdiction over federal housing and urban renewal programs, and the Public Works Committee, which has jurisdiction over river and harbor projects and federal building and land acquisition as well as the highway program, that no federal or federally aided property acquisition met the real needs of those directly affected. I also learned that relocation assistance varied from one program to another. Some of the most tragic stories related to urban renewal, where federal money was being used to wipe out slums and other forms of urban blight.

Eyesores were being destroyed, but the people who lived in the slums often found that they had no place to go.

The facts about these injustices were not hard to find, and the legislation was not hard to draft. But it took over five years to get the legislation through the Senate and the House of Representatives and to get the President to sign it. Resistance dies hard to requirements that may slow down building in order to meet the needs of people who haven't much power. More than a year after President Nixon signed the Act, his administration still hadn't issued the guidelines to put the program to work.

We have been so busy remaking the surface of our land and the shape of our communities that we have often failed to take time to see how those changes are affecting us and to think before we put the bulldozers in motion. That has been one of my major concerns as chairman of the Subcommittee on Air and Water Pollution. It has also occupied my attention as chairman of the Subcommittee on Intergovernmental Relations. As I looked at various proposals to reform grant-in-aid programs, and as I worked on urban-planning programs on the Senate Banking and Currency Committee, I found that there was almost no way in metropolitan areas for citizens in one community to affect decisions in other communities that would have a great impact on them. Highway programs that benefited suburban communities were destroying the economic and social viability of the inner city, but city governments had no way to influence highway construction outside their jurisdiction, except in those few instances where healthy working relationships had developed as part of regional planning programs. I tried to help that trend along by legislation that supported regional councils of governments, made up of elected officials from different communities in metropolitan areas, but I knew that the federal government would have to play a more active role in requiring reviews of projects supported by federal funds if we were to cut across city and county lines to give communities a chance to protect themselves against damage from big construction programs. My proposal ran into opposition from big-city and suburban spokesmen, each of whom was afraid of having pet projects blocked by the other side. The biggest obstacle, however, turned out to be federal officials whose wings might be clipped in the review process. Their concerns were reflected in different congressional committees.

There seemed to be no hope of getting the legislation passed until the late spring of 1966, when President Johnson asked me to manage the Demonstration Cities Act. I liked his objective and I wanted to do what I could to shift the focus of our urban programs from bricks and mortar to human needs, but I had problems with some of the details of the legislation, and I had strong doubts as to our ability to get the legislation through the Congress. I told him I would agree to take on the assignment if I could satisfy myself on those two points. My staff worked up some proposed changes in the legislation, including the addition of the metropolitan review requirements I had tried to get through the Congress without success. I thought that was an important proposal to complement some of the inner-city features of the legislation. In a sense, it was part of my price for getting the President's package through the Senate. The Administration agreed, and metropolitan-wide review of important public development projects became a part of national policy. It was another example of how legislative compromise can sometimes mean an advance, not a retreat, from a previous position. That move also illustrated how intertwined the concerns of different congressional committees can be. I was struggling with the problem of how highways, airports, mass transit systems, sewage treatment plants, solid waste disposal facilities, urban renewal projects, and hospitals can affect an individual citizen living on the other side of the city line from the project. And that problem revealed itself in the work of three separate committees on which I served. Putting the pieces together took time, ingenuity and, in the end, some leverage on the White House, which is all part of making the system work.

David Broder once wrote, in a review of a book called *Muskie*,* that the real question in my candidacy and in what I stand for is whether traditional institutions and some of the old, recognizable values can be made to yield solutions to the problems that confront us. I think that the Senate, like some of our other institutions, can and at times does work remarkably well. We also need reform, in the Senate as elsewhere in the nation, and that is always true of institutions. You can't always be sure that today's reforms will meet tomorrow's needs, although we are usually sure that today's reforms would have met yesterday's. That sort of ironic dilemma is in the nature of political processes. It is like progress: Everyone is for it. The only difference is that liberals are for tomorrow's progress and conservatives are all for yesterday's progress.

There is some reason to believe that the center in American politics has been moving to the left. When Social Security was enacted in 1935, only one Republican voted for it. In 1964, a conservative Republican candidate was defeated, in part, because people thought he was against Social Security, although he denied the charge vehemently. That represents quite a change in American political life, and the

* Hansen, Donald C., and Lippman, Theodore, *Muskie*, New York, W. W. Norton & Company, Inc., 1971.

Senate, although it sometimes seems monolithic or unbending, is quite loose and adaptable.

Before I came to the Senate I thought of it as a place where chairmen of committees use their powers to bottle up constructive legislation. I soon learned that this is the exception, and not the rule. The late Willis Robertson of Virginia, for example, was a very conservative southern senator and chairman of the Banking and Currency Commission when I arrived. A lot of far-reaching liberal housing legislation came out of that committee while he was chairman. Willis always voted against it, yet he never tried to stop it. That would not have been true fifty or probably thirty years ago. A committee chairman would have been controlling.

Lyndon Johnson was responsible for many of the changes in the Senate, including a speed-up in the handling of legislation. He made a change in Senate procedures that isn't found in the rules, isn't found in the books anywhere, and yet is the single most important change that has taken place since I have been in the Senate. That is the unanimous consent procedure for bypassing the Senate rules tradition. We still have unlimited debate; yet if we were to assert that right in the case of all legislation we would have to stay here ten years to do one year's work. Johnson developed the idea of getting unanimous consent to limit debate to a specific time so that we could dispose of legislation in an hour or a couple of hours or a day. By astutely developing that policy and not using it to run over people or to abuse their rights, it has worked. Mike Mansfield uses it in the same way. He is able to get senators to agree to unanimous consent to limit the time on debate. It is especially effective in the closing days when we have a great deal of legislation to finish. Devised in an *ad hoc* way, it has now become a traditional part of Senate procedure.

That loosening up of Senate operations should provide some insight into the complexity of Lyndon Johnson and the institution he knew so well. In my Senate years I learned to work with Mr. Johnson, as Majority Leader, Vice-President, and President. We never had a comfortable relationship, but it was productive, particularly on domestic issues.

For most of the rest of my first year in the Senate, after our clash on the filibuster rule, Senator Johnson hardly spoke to me. Later in the year, when he learned that I was going to Puerto Rico for a Governors Conference to discuss legislation, he invited me into his office and asked me to take some political soundings. He was already interested in the 1960 presidential sweepstakes. He was interested in my serving his political purpose to whatever extent I might be willing. At least we were on a talking basis after that. But while he was Majority Leader ours was always a cool relationship.

He liked to have people flocking around his banner and playing up to him. At the same time he understood a senator's right to independence, and he respected those senators who were independent. He also liked to have men with whom he could reason and who were willing to give him support on key issues. The more they were willing to support him, the more he would appreciate them and was ready to reciprocate. He didn't require toadying as such.

My visit to Puerto Rico involved a little case history that is instructive. At about that time, President Eisenhower had vetoed a housing bill. The Senate was considering whether to override the veto or to put together a new bill that would come closer to President Eisenhower's specifications. I was a member of the Banking and Currency Committee and the question of a veto was referred to that committee. The Sub-committee on Housing was to vote while I was away in Puerto Rico. I told the chairman, Senator Sparkman, that I preferred writing a new bill to overriding and that I hoped he would cast my proxy for that course. When I went into the Majority Leader's office to discuss the Puerto Rican trip, Lyndon got into the question of the housing bill, which was high on his agenda. I told him that the subcommittee would act while I was gone, and that I had left my proxy with John Sparkman to support a new bill. He said, "That's right. Good. That coincides with my judgment."

I went to Puerto Rico for two or three days. When I came back, I read in the New York *Times* that the sub-committee had acted the day before and that my proxy had been cast to override the veto.

I called Sparkman: "What happened?"

"Well," he said, "we had enough votes to go the other way without your vote and since the subcommittee had voted to write a new bill, I thought that coming from your part of the country you'd be better off politically if your vote went to override." I said, "John, that doesn't happen to be the case, but whether it is or not, you've got me in trouble with the Majority Leader again."

He laughed. "Oh, I know. He's already called me. So I explained and it's all right."

When I went in to give Lyndon my report on Puerto Rico, I wanted to make sure that he understood what had happened on the veto vote. He said that he understood. "The bill is now in full committee," I said. "I'm leaving for Maine, but I'm leaving my proxy behind and I still want to vote for a new bill and against overriding."

"Right," he said, "exactly what we ought to do."

Coming back from Maine, we landed briefly in Boston, and while on the ground I got a message that there was a phone call from the Majority Leader. I rushed into the terminal but couldn't get him on the phone. When the plane stopped in New York, they told me that there was a call from the Majority Leader. So I called back again and this time we connected.

"Ed? Ed, I thought you ought to know that we cast your vote in the committee to override the veto."

"You did?" I said. "Now why in the hell did you do that?"

"I got up this morning," Lyndon said, "and that —— Drew Pearson, had a column about how we were playing around with this thing and we decided, by God, we're going to override this veto and I needed your vote."

That is the way Lyndon manipulated votes. He was totally absorbed in the job, twenty-four hours a day. He was unhappy with that Pearson column and he didn't take much very lightly anyhow. If you lived around him, worked closely with him, you felt that all-consuming quality. It was better from my point of view to stand a little apart, to keep a slight distance, without the coolness and unpleasantness with which we had started. I admired tremendously the way he kept that Senate moving. He did a remarkable job, getting work turned out on schedule, getting results, getting the results he wanted. He didn't have his easy majority all the time. He had to split votes with liberals and conservatives. There was grumbling from all quarters. The liberals thought he was using them and that he didn't give them enough attention, but he understood what many didn't—that he had nowhere else to go. The votes were to be won in one place, the Senate, not elsewhere, so he leaned on them, and got them all, liberals, conservatives, Republicans, Southerners. He knew that he could count on the liberals because often what he proposed to do moved in their direction. If he didn't go as far as they wanted, he still would give them more than the Republicans would give. It was astute, practical leadership.

Lyndon differed from Mike Mansfield, his successor, in many ways. One was his willingness to get us to work evenings and Saturdays, to get legislation out and on schedule. There were times, however, when he resorted to stalling. I remember that in 1960, the year of the convention, we would have been through by the Fourth of July—except that in the last week of June Lyndon decided for his own political purposes that we had better not wind up the session. He wanted us to come back after the convention. That would be his forum for running against Vice-President Nixon. If it hadn't been for that, we could have been all through for the year, by the Fourth.

Lyndon hoped to get the nomination, but Jack Kennedy was ahead at that point, ahead in delegate count, in momentum, in public acceptance. Kennedy never faltered, and Lyndon's carefully laid plan for the postconvention session went for naught.

Lyndon lacked sophistication on the national scene. He felt that senators were leaders, important wielders of political power in their states. And this is not usually the case. The U. S. Senate had been his life, his political life, and it was the source of *his* power. I suppose, therefore, that he sometimes assumed it was the source of all political power. It was his one major political instinct, and responses and sensitivities that might have tided him over or carried him through some of the crises in the Senate finally brought him down in the presidency.

He was always a Senate man. His great achievements as President were in legislative action. This was his field. He knew how to do it, how to get legislation moving, and how to get it out. He knew how to compromise and how to use and find the right senators and the right bills. In this, he was pre-eminent. There has never been legislative production like his in the history of the republic because this is where he knew what he was doing. But outside Washington, I don't think he ever was as effective a political leader as he hoped and believed.

The descriptions of President Johnson as the consummate political "animal" are imprecise. Columnists in their early evaluations of Kennedy and Johnson described him as such, over and over again. Once he won election to the presidency in his own right, then he was supposed to be the ultimate political king.

The same sort of things have been written about President Nixon. He lost in 1960, he lost the California governorship in 1962. Yet once he won the presidency he became the consummate national politician. It is success that writes the label. Actually, a loser often has more useful political insights and perspectives than a winner (and, further, he has time to think things out), but having lost, he is obviously not an expert in the eyes of some beholders. Despite the great margin of victory in 1964, I never believed that Johnson was an effective national politician. Many things he did in the early stages of the presidency he assumed represented a skillful molding of public opinion, an avoidance of his own weaknesses, and an enhancement of his strengths. But if political skill is demonstrated by sensitivity to people who shape public opinion, and to those who *are* public opinion, who get things moving along political lines on a national basis, then I don't believe he was a superpolitician, as sometimes painted.

His great technical (if that is the word) weakness was his inability to use television effectively. He worked hard at it, seeking to find a voice or a tone or style. But he never did master the medium as effectively as some of us would have liked. He took to using the East Room of the White House for television speeches, a more manageable room than the President's office for him. He had a special TV podium built there, with invisible prompters, and hardware and paraphernalia developed to give him the appearance of being released from the mechanics of TV, to help give him the appearance of being relaxed and informal. But he was uneasy in front of that camera, and he couldn't read a speech well from a prepared text. There was a stiffness about it all. Toward the end, he did manage to loosen up and he made a couple of good appearances, but by that time his credibility had been so undermined that there wasn't much he could do about it.

On the other hand, one theme that he developed immediately after the assassination of John Kennedy was that of continuity. It was reassuring, healthy, necessary, and he did it beautifully. It was instinctive. It promised great things. He kept Kennedy people on, and there was staging in the consultations with the Secretary of State, with the heads of government who came here. He had a constant round of things moving, government in motion, to document, to illustrate his theme. His first message to the Congress began with the ringing "We shall continue . . ."

He drove that continuity theme home, he knew that it was vital to the country and to the world, vital to demonstrate the durability of our institutions and the stability of our society and our political mechanism. He *did* continue, and he followed through on the Kennedy program; he took maximum advantage of the political power that grew around the Kennedy name in the bleak, somber, inspiring time after the assassination. The Senate know-how and the Kennedy clout came together, but the success of the continuity effort came from his own deep conviction and commitment to the American system and our political institutions. It was an instinctive theme, but he couldn't have chosen a better one; it led to the successful year in office before his nomination and landslide victory.

The same-time period also produced the decisions on the war that ultimately turned against him. Some key decisions had been pending for President Kennedy, and there were more waiting for President Johnson. The adviser program in Vietnam hadn't worked; there was political instability in South Vietnam. At the time of his death, President Kennedy was facing the decision about whether to increase American involvement further or to cut it off. I don't think it was that simple, but that was the issue on the desk, and Lyndon Johnson, not having the benefit of whatever doubts President Kennedy might have had in his own mind, tied the war into the continuity theme.

John Kennedy had, after all, increased the advisers from something less than a thousand to sixteen thousand, and so, I suppose, the new President felt he had to continue to follow through. He could not go back on a commitment made by his predecessor.

He had never been belligerent about the war. In fact, he had been very cool to the idea of increased American involvement in the French effort. Escalating the war was not, I think, instinctive for him. It must have been, in considerable part, a function of his respect for his principal advisers, men like Dean Rusk and Robert McNamara. What did belong to him, I believe, was his view of the war. He saw it, I

suspect, as comparable to a piece of legislation. He seemed
to treat war almost as if it were a work that could be accomplished by compromise, by amendment, an act that you could
control. For instance, once when I was critical of the bombing because it was so destructive of civilian life, though the
bombs were intended for military targets, he said: "Ed,
I've got a bombsight there, you know, one we can really pinpoint the target with. . . ."

Always, as I watched him, I had the feeling that he
believed what he was saying and what he had been told. He
believed that the bombs could be dropped with absolute
precision and totally controlled effect, taking out military
targets, just as you might strike out a comma here or a period
there, or add a sentence or take one away in the drafting of
legislation. It was an almost surgical view. You could eliminate the problem over there if you simply did this or that.
He treated the Indochina problem, which in fact involved
people and their lives and their reactions, in a strange, unin-
tended kind of impersonal way. He always seemed to feel
that you could manage the war as you would steer a piece of
legislation, if you just got the right people to handle it, the
right committee to move. If you had the facts, you could put
together a "package" that would contain the war, that would
limit the human and the financial burden. I think this very
familiar feeling, that the President was managing it, sold the
Congress into feeling that . . . well, yes, Lyndon can manage it. There was really little disquiet about it, even through
the Tonkin Gulf resolution. Only two senators voted against
it: Senators Wayne Morse and Ernest Gruening.

Tonkin Gulf was, we have been told, the legislative authority for all that followed in American involvement. We
never regarded it that way, never saw it as being quite that
embracing, we didn't focus on the consequences that might

flow . . . even Senator Fulbright did not. There was the
sense that "This guy, you know, when he has a problem,
he can manage it. . . ."

He didn't manage it, and neither did we. To a certain
extent, President Johnson—and most of us—shared the American feeling that all problems are solvable, all objectives
reachable, that given enough time, talent, and money, we can
lick anything. Johnson in a very real way was a reflection of
our American attitude about good old Yankee know-how.
In certain respects he did remarkably well. With the war he—
and we—did not. We staggered deeper and deeper into a
crisis that was a product of the cold war, our involvement in
Vietnam, and a symptom of deeper, long-term problems at
home that we had ignored or glossed over.

The crisis, those problems, and the presidential campaign
of 1968 came together in a way that was fateful for many of
us.

CHAPTER II

•

The 1968 Campaign and After

THOUGH THE CAMPAIGN began for me with President Johnson's speech, the political implications didn't sink in very quickly. I thought first of its possible impact on the war. My wife and I talked of its personal effect on the President and Mrs. Johnson.

By the next morning, of course, it was the talk of the country, and I can't recall that even then my thoughts were distinctly different from those of anyone else.

In what would seem to be very short order we would go from a situation in which we had an incumbent President who would surely run again, to one in which there was a race, and a widening one at that. Senator McCarthy was in; Senator Robert Kennedy would be in before long; the President was out; and the Vice-President had to make some quick decisions. Most surprising to me, perhaps, was that I would be in, too.

It is not that the idea of the vice-presidency had never crossed my mind. (Or, as an American boy brought up with all the proper beliefs, that I had never dreamed, at least briefly, that I too could be President.) But I had done no lobbying for such a nomination. Mrs. Johnson's book* indicates that I had been considered a candidate for the vice-presidential nomination in 1964, and the idea had been at least mentioned in 1960. But President Johnson never discussed the thought with me. People whose advice he sought about my eligibility did tell me of their discussions with the President, however.

On April 4, 1968, there was a Democratic Congressional Campaign Dinner at the Washington Hilton. Vice-President Humphrey was there, representing the President, and I was the chairman of the Senate Campaign Committee. A master of ceremonies started the evening's program and it was under way when someone came in with the word that the Reverend Martin Luther King, Jr., had been shot in Memphis.

As the word spread through the room, the master of ceremonies continued with the program. He had launched into one of those old-fashioned, hard-hitting political stump speeches, very much out of tune with the mood of the audience. Each of us was shocked and stunned. It was obvious to me what had to be done. I spoke to Congressman Mike Kirwan, who was chairman of the Democratic Congressional Campaign Committee, and with the Vice-President, and we found ourselves in agreement. I stepped up to the podium and, I am afraid, pushed the MC aside and

* Johnson, Lady Bird, *White House Diary*, New York, Holt, Rinehart & Winston, Inc., 1970.

announced that the dinner was over. There would be no more politics, no more speeches, no more entertainment. The Vice-President would say a few words about Doctor King but, after that, the evening was ended.

As we left the hotel, Hubert and Muriel Humphrey invited Jane and me, our daughter Ellen, and our son Steve to their apartment. We were sobered and quiet for a time. We spoke of the assassination and its possible origin and consequences. Later, when the talk touched on politics, I encouraged Hubert to run.

In Washington, one can never avoid politics entirely. The fact that the Vice-President and I had left the dinner together touched off speculation in the press. The truth is that we did not discuss my possible involvement that night.

As events unfolded, I continued to think that the Vice-President should run. My relationship with Gene McCarthy was of somewhat longer standing, and after Robert Kennedy entered the race, he had to be considered seriously, as well.

I didn't think of McCarthy or Kennedy as divisive forces. Even though Gene had won by a sort of consensus in the New Hampshire primary (actually he hadn't, but that was the impression he wanted us to have and the reaction he got), he still had, in my judgment, a long way to go toward building a national political following that would be large enough to win the presidency over Richard Nixon who, I thought, would turn out to be the Republican nominee. On balance, I thought that Hubert would have the best chance of holding our fragmenting party together, and in mobilizing and winning the election.

Later in April, Hubert Humphrey did announce his candidacy. This news, welcome to many of us, was somewhat tempered by his use of the phrase "the politics of joy." Undoubtedly, the Vice-President believed that political life and action could be, and probably should be, a joyous experience and that this nation was capable again of enjoying its political system. But the mood and the hour were wrong. The death of Martin Luther King, the vehemence over Vietnam, and other episodes all conspired against any feeling of good humor, not to say joy.

In the middle of May, Vice-President Hubert Humphrey and I flew to Maine to address the state Democratic convention.

We have almost all forgotten, now, how difficult that decision was for Hubert Humphrey and, once made, how little time there was to raise money to organize, to do any kind of first-rate job. We have forgotten how far behind Hubert Humphrey was when he decided to run.

In the plane, I told Hubert that we would be uncommitted in Maine. We would work for a favorite-son position at the state convention, to keep our people together, to avoid splitting, and I said that I would be publicly noncommittal in the interest of that objective.

On that flight north, the Vice-President for the first time got into the subject of his running mate. He said that what he wanted was a man who could take over the presidency if necessary, and a man who would be a close confidante and adviser to the President. I think he meant it. It was natural that, in contemplating the awesome responsibility he sought, he should think also of wanting that right man with him. He was himself the kind of man who took seriously the chilling lessons we had learned about succession after the illness of President Eisenhower and the assassination of President Kennedy.

The second spot on the ticket was obviously uppermost in his mind at a time when he had severe political problems which might have made any consideration of a running mate very secondary. That he would be talking, even obliquely, to an obscure senator from Maine about the vice-presidential nomination was an indication that he must have been deeply concerned.

He said that I was high on his list. He indicated that, if he had a personal choice, I would be his choice. He didn't say this in so many words but that was the evident implication.

During the late spring and into June and July, I watched Humphrey picking up delegates. Despite difficulties, one could see him building up support. After the death of Robert Kennedy, there was no other sure alternative and I began to be concerned and said so. I felt that his organization was not planning for the campaign after the convention. The focus ought to be on how to deal with Mr. Nixon, the most likely Republican nominee.

In August, I appeared before the Platform Committee in Washington, made a number of recommendations on domestic policy, and called for a bombing halt in stronger terms than I had ever used. President Johnson had suspended bombing north of the 19th parallel but I asked for further risks in pursuit of peace and for a complete end to the bombing strikes.

That proposal received some favorable attention in the press. An editorial in the Washington *Post* said in part:

> The Democrats may not be able to perfect a compromise Vietnam plank that will satisfy both sides, but if they do it will surely be reached by conforming to the temper and tendency of Sen. Edmund Muskie's testimony before the resolutions committee. . . . Apart from the substantive essentials of his proposals, the temper and tone of his approach is deserving of the highest commendation. He may not have succeeded in elim-

inating honest differences but he has demonstrated a
method of dealing with these differences without running a fever or falling prey to hysteria.†

Soon, we were off to Illinois where, I hoped, we would
meet and mend.

There was more than one story in Chicago that summer,
of course, and mine was not the important one. There was
the preconvention period and the work on planks and platform, and procedures. There was the role of the absent
President. There was the war in Vietnam. And there was
the war in the streets outside. The stories were related, but
they were also quite separate. Yet in the world of television,
the stories were run together until they seemed to be one.

I was to have no special role at the convention itself and
nothing to do with its operation. The Maine delegation
never did nominate me as favorite son because that was a
move I had accepted at our state convention only for the
purpose of buying time, to allow our delegates to make up
their minds about the announced candidates. I was never
particularly interested in a favorite-son nomination on the
floor. So before the convention opened, when I thought our
delegates had gained ample time to consider the candidates
carefully, I flew out to Chicago, held a press conference
announcing my support of Vice-President Humphrey, and
released the Maine delegation.

The week of the convention, the Vice-President did ask
my help on the Vietnam war plank for the party platform.
The objective was to try to soften it, to modify it, and recon-
cile those who wanted the war ended immediately with
those who supported the Administration's conviction that we

† The Washington *Post*, August 21, 1968.

could not withdraw at that point. I even asked Chicago's Mayor Daley to intercede with President Johnson.

Nobody sent me to see Daley. I hadn't had much contact with him over the years. As chairman of the Senate Subcommittee on Intergovernmental Relations, I had him testify several times before that subcommittee and before the Advisory Commission on Intergovernmental Relations. His testimony was always useful, especially when he departed from his text and we got into hard questions and answers on the problems of the cities, including racial ones. He always talked with me after testifying and I had dropped in to see him in Chicago as a courtesy. But I did not discuss the convention or candidates in detail with him; it just occurred to me that since I had read and heard about his close relationship with President Johnson, we ought to try to ask him to help in softening the President on the war plank. He said that he didn't discuss substantive questions with Lyndon Johnson. He didn't feel the President would listen to him on the subject, and he didn't think he was competent to discuss the nuances of the several planks.

It was late in the day when I was asked to help develop a platform, and any changes we could achieve were minimal, but I felt an obligation to try. What we would accomplish was chiefly in interpretation. Because we couldn't get the language changed much, Wilson Wyatt, who had been Adlai Stevenson's campaign manager in 1952 and was an active member of the Platform Committee, and I agreed that I would start off the debate on the plank, and he would end it. Thus, we would try to leave a final imprint on the majority plank that would permit us to take to the country a stand that was consistent with ending the war, including taking steps to include the cessation of all bombing. But I had the feeling throughout that speakers on all sides hadn't fully read the planks we were debating. In some cases they used the debate as a forum for advancing their own views and for "exposure," but the labors of those who worked to try to contain and rationalize the explosive forces present were ultimately helpful. Much of the debate was useful, not only politically; it advanced the Democrats toward new positions following the convention, positions that could help solve the immensely agonizing issue of the war.

The debate went largely uncovered on television. The networks covered a few of the statements, but only in bits and pieces, despite the fact that such a substantial debate on a thorny, vital issue had few precedents in the history of conventions. This sort of genuine soul-searching and intellectual effort had not gone on since the 1948 debate on the civil rights plank. As Democrats, we agreed that we had a problem and a serious division that we were prepared to argue out in public, rather than trying to paper it over.

When one considers the shattering of the party earlier in the year, the tragedy in the death of Robert Kennedy, of the ended McCarthy candidacy, of the President's withdrawal, when all of that and more is reviewed, the fact that the party held a convention at all—without violence in the meeting itself and with a rules change that had the effect of permanently liberalizing the convention in the representation of delegations—is surprising. It was an accomplishment for the Democrats, but even more for the democratic process.

Inside the hall, old processes were being refined and improved. Outside in the streets, the old order was being torn up.

If you looked at the convention from the perspective of the young anti-war demonstrators who gathered, and who must have felt so frustrated there in Lincoln Park, the convention surely appeared to be a repressive, rough, tough,

irresponsible operation. From the point of view of those
who were trying to run a convention inside the hall, or of
those unsympathetic to the demonstrators, the chaos and the
pain and distress produced outside made it appear that the dis-
rupters were rough and irresponsible and were trying to
repress a political process.

What happened on the streets of Chicago, on all sides,
was saddening, maddening, depressing. We didn't invite the
disturbances, though I suppose by the mere fact of our lawful
assembly we must have been a magnet, nor did we ask for or
approve all the methods used to restore order. But the convention and the chaos happened concurrently, and the world
saw them as cause and effect. The results, for young
people injured and for policemen insulted and degraded,
were appalling and in due course we paid the price.

With the separate episodes in Chicago reduced to one by
television's omnipresent cameras and by cutting back and
forth, a viewer saw a drama in which Mayor Richard Daley
seemed to be directing both the convention and the police
outside. One would have thought that he had moment-to-
moment, day-to-day control of the convention. He was, of
course, the controlling force in one of the largest delegations,
that of Illinois, a delegation strategically situated in the convention hall, right in front of the podium. As the cameras
revealed, he had very definite views about what was going
on, about the people who were speaking, and what they were
saying. Those views were expressed facially and by gesture. I remember the cameras catching one movement, a
hand across the throat, which suggested that he was com-
manding Chairman Carl Albert to recess a session of the
convention. Actually, that decision had already been made.
Carl was in the process of recessing when Mayor Daley
made the gesture. The picture, much reproduced, tended to
"document" the Mayor's tight control over the convention.

Daley was indeed an influence—in fact, speculation swirled around all week on what was happening between him and the Teddy Kennedy forces. But anybody who knows Carl Albert also knows that you don't control him.

There is no doubt in my mind that the convention was one of the biggest obstacles to our winning. We almost overcame it, but not quite.

At about four o'clock in the afternoon of the last day of the convention, I was notified that Hubert had made his decision. My acceptance speech had to be written for delivery between 7 and 8 P.M.—so we had to have it ready for reproducing and release at 6. But before anything, I had to notify Jane. She had been waiting all day at the Conrad Hilton.

Jane's reaction was one of acceptance. I think we both felt letdown or relief; a decision had been made. We were subdued by the awareness of the responsibilities involved and of the magnitude of the job that lay ahead for both of us, win or lose. She had accepted the possibility. Now that it was a fact, I knew that *her* acceptance speech, the most important one, had been made to me a long time ago—and I was grateful. So we went about the business of getting our clothes together for the appearance that evening.

As we moved toward the convention, the nominations for Vice-President opened. Inside the hall, I noticed that the California delegation wasn't even in attendance. Then there was the nomination of Julian Bond. This was an understandable nomination, but under the Constitution he was not old enough to qualify. Amid all the confusion and controversy and hasty consultations, I didn't have any concern that my nomination would be blocked. Finally, it was done.

The key acceptance speech was, naturally, Hubert Humphrey's. Oddly enough, though he had won the nomination fairly and was one of the most popular Democrats alive, it took real courage for Hubert to face that audience and to try to rally it for the campaign ahead. For my part, I knew that my own talk would be anti-climactic, even though it would precede Hubert's, and so I thought it should be brief and to the point. I had been disturbed for some time, as many people had, about the growing divisions within the country, the questions of race, of war, of protest, of the system itself. I had been developing that theme quietly, using it in commencement addresses.

Perhaps there is cynicism about high school commencement speeches, but I always take them seriously—and so, perhaps, if any of the young people who had listened to me at their school saw me at the convention, they might have been surprised to find whole elements of my talk which were familiar. Some of my staff thought what I had in mind would be too sober, some thought it was out of the tradition of acceptance speeches, and several thought it ought to be more of a cheerleading, rousing blast. I didn't think so. And that kind of performance takes longer to give than just coming out and saying what is on your mind.

A cheerleading speech, in any case, would not have worked, given the noise on the floor, the public address system, and the spirit in the air. I had tried to think of something to say at first that might help break the tension. So I told them that I had called my mother at home in Maine right after I had been selected. But she knew already; the reporters had arrived. I asked my sisters what their reactions had been. And they said that when my mother was asked whether or not she would vote for me, her reply was: "Well, if nobody better comes along."

I think her response helped clear the stormy, smoky air of that convention hall.

My mother is very frank, in fact, blunt at times. Most people learn to take her comments with a grain of salt. But some take her at her word, which can be dangerous and sometimes backfires. I know that when a magazine writer reported that my mother liked my younger brother better than me, she was hurt. My mother meant that Eugene was jollier and more outgoing, while I was quieter and more serious, and so he was more fun. My mother treated us all alike, which is to say fairly. She would divide a candy bar into six equal pieces, rather than play favorites or risk an injustice. Her comments are sometimes less than judicial, but I think that her bluntness is refreshing.

My aim in that speech was not so much at the people on the floor; it was at the national audience.

The part that I lifted almost bodily out of the commencement-style speech was one in which I said that we had to learn to live with our differences:

To make a society such as ours work is not easy. It means learning to live with, to understand and to respect many different kinds of human beings, of different colors, of different races, or different national origins, of different cultural levels, of different tastes and intellectual capacities, of different educational attainments, of different social backgrounds, personalities and dispositions, and to accept them all as equals.

It means learning to trust each other, to work with each other, to think of each other as neighbors. It means diminishing our prerogatives by as much as is necessary to give others the same prerogatives. It means respect for the rule of law as a dispenser of justice as well as a maintainer of order.

I had, as it turned out, enunciated, without quite realizing it, the central theme of the campaign to come.

Hubert's acceptance speech was courageous, I thought, and it was well received.

Afterward, there was a victory celebration with the Maine delegation. Jane and I were with them for forty-five minutes or an hour. Then we went back to the hotel and listened to the postconvention analyses of the television correspondents. I thought they were a little rough on us, but there had been a lot of roughness that week and they, no more than we, had much perspective at that point. Their comments didn't exactly add a cheery note to the week's end; instead, they helped to highlight the rocks on the road that faced us. When I went to bed that night, it was not with any glow of triumph.

The day after the convention we went to Minnesota with the Humphreys to their beloved Waverly. It was to be our only respite until after the election. From the hotel in Chicago to O'Hare Airport we had a heavy escort of Secret Service agents, local police, and army helicopters. It was a final reminder of the threat of violence that hung over the city. We boarded the plane, and with a sense of relief we flew off to Minneapolis, and then drove to Waverly and the Humphreys' lakeside home. Jane and I stayed in a rustic, comfortable cottage which reminded us of the camps in Maine we had enjoyed over the years. We rested, talked, and delighted in Hubert's proud display of his vacation spot. There was little time spent on the details of the campaign.

At the end of that couple of days, Hubert unleashed us to set up our travel plans and organization. My campaign staff went ahead and leased an airplane. The press who would travel with us paid their share, and we raised the rest of the money and ran our part of the campaign in the black.

As we co-ordinated campaign schedules, we recognized early that I could not go into every state. The plan was for me to go into states where I was likely to do the most good. It was understandable that I should be assigned the "ethnic areas," but I went not to sell an ethnic message but simply as a spokesman who would be accepted to discuss the issues. I enjoyed talking with and for minority groups—I am, after all, part of one myself. But I felt then and do now that there should be no appeals made to our differences if the cost is to tear the nation apart.

There is confusion in our land about whether the United States is a melting pot, or whether we are an unaligned, disunited assortment of racial, religious, and ethnic elements. The truth lies, as it often does, somewhere in between. For a long time we had the conviction that what we were accomplishing here was a new breed, The American, and that somehow he or she was going to be a composite of all the groups. After some evolutionary period, this figure called The American would emerge with all the previous differences submerged or assimilated in him. It was an appealing picture; there was a heroic quality to it, the sort of thing that evidenced itself in our Olympic-game heroes and in our technological achievements . . . a breed of stronger people, physically better developed, better educated, more idealistic than anyone who had gone before. In other words, we were distilling all the best in all the people with the less desirable qualities being consumed or eliminated. This ideal lurked in the background for the immigrants who came here, for the disadvantaged in the nation, and behind many public policies. We sought to create the kind of environment that would provide a suitable home for this kind of American.

We have now begun to understand that we cannot just wipe away our differences, that the differences add to the richness of our culture. The idea of a smooth new breed without differences is no service either to America or to the component groups of this country. In our time, these groups have focused on the fact that they make their own contributions from their cultures, traditions, history, and values, and that these are important. They believe, and I believe, that many contrasts, much "differentness," ought to be kept alive, and encouraged and cultivated, not buried or melted away in a pot. Black Americans have helped to stimulate other groups to pride in their own contributions.

Once we recognize our differences and the worth of them, rather than the trouble they cause, they become easier to live with. We no longer have to feel that anything uncomfortable or unfamiliar or even unpleasant must be swept away. Against the polar ideas of either eradicating differences or of proclaiming independent antagonistic states is a more livable concept. We can not only tolerate each other but we can learn to appreciate the richness we draw from each other. If we can fix on that reality, then we will go further in building a new kind of country, not a single new America but an America which is more human, more stimulating and yet comfortable, more broadminded—a country which does not demand the breeding of supermen.

On the Sunday following the convention I got an invitation to Texas. We had done a "Meet the Press" program in Minneapolis, which apparently had a wide audience. A call came into the studio from a man who urged me to come to the Hemisfair in San Antonio. He wanted me to participate in what was, in effect, Polish-American Day. That was the only good invitation we had at that point. Hemisfair had some possibilities: presumably a good-sized audience, a visit to the Alamo—even a chance to make a speech in front of the Alamo. That was as good a start as a politician could hope for, and we could do it right away.

I had never been to San Antonio. In fact, I really hadn't been to Texas much. It turned out to be a full day. The weather was really hot. It was still a tough job holding the Alamo; after an hour in that torrid square every stitch of our clothing was wet.

I was immediately conscious of the fact that Muskie was hardly a well-known name. Attendance was sparse by the standards of a national ticket, but the people were as warm as the day was hot and as we traveled around the Hemisfair folks were reasonably receptive. There was even some enthusiasm. The Polish-American affair wasn't well attended, but a few hundred people gathered there.

Later, there was a reception, and there was a Democratic Party dinner that night, with a packed hall and a bright reception.

The reporters with us were curious. They didn't know what kind of candidate they were going to cover; they were puzzled and eventually bothered that my speeches didn't give them much of a lead, a complaint which issued for some time after that. Until an event in Washington, Pennsylvania, they were increasingly bored, I suspect.

The incident in Washington, Pennsylvania, was probably the turning point in the campaign, at least for my part of it. We were several weeks into the campaign itself. We had been busy, had found a reasonable reception in many places, although nothing really dramatic or spectacular happened. I thought we were building slowly.

I had a good press in papers around the country, but there was little attention paid in the New York *Times* or the Washington *Post*. Any upswing or interest in my candidacy

would have to be based on that coverage in the hinterlands—which are hinterlands only if you live in Washington
or New York. We didn't have money for television, so we
tried to take advantage of the hospitality of the local talk
shows. There are a lot of them and they have sizable local
audiences, with more impact, really, in some areas than the
national programs. I made a point of participating in as
many of those as possible. These had, I think, an influence
on further invitations for both Vice-President Humphrey and
for me. In turn, this eventually contributed to his movement
upward in the polls, which then began to have national
repercussions. No one has ever satisfactorily explained why
that initial upward movement took place. We hadn't had
any national television impact to speak of and didn't have
much in the way of literature. We traveled for weeks, for
example, without even bumper stickers to distribute. We had
no piece of paper with my photograph on it, or biography or
campaign biography.

Slowly, the local TV and newspaper interviews that both
Hubert and I enjoyed began to have their effect. The local
shows are perhaps the equivalent of the old whistle-stop
campaign. And it is not just television; it is radio, too, local
radio, which people hear in their cars and housewives listen
to in the kitchen. This coverage is important.

On one particular grueling day, we went from West Virginia into Pennsylvania and then on to Michigan. One leg
of the trip meant a drive from Pittsburgh to Washington,
Pennsylvania, as part of a tour through some of the towns
around Pittsburgh. I think Washington was the second or
third stop of the day. A speech was scheduled for noon
at the County Courthouse, and before that we sat down to
lunch at the George Washington Hotel across the way.

While eating, we learned that a group of hostile students,

some from nearby Washington and Jefferson College, had gathered in front of the platform. I sensed that this was to be my first big "confrontation."

I hadn't had much of this sort of thing before, although Hubert had been having some very unpleasant times.

For many students, the defeat of Senator Eugene McCarthy was the defeat of their hero. The student protest was concentrated on Hubert Humphrey, as a symbol of the Democratic Party. At the University of San Francisco, one week before, the students had walked out on the Vice-President. Earlier, I had given thought to what one might say to students, and how to deal with them. One way of doing it struck me. I had suggested it to the Vice-President in one of our evening talks. He thought well of it, so I waited to see whether or not he would use the idea, but he didn't. When I got to the moment, I knew I had a possible answer, and in any case I now had the problem, too.

We had to move across the square through the gathering crowd, including the students. It was not a very easy moment. The students seemed to be in an ugly mood, and as I moved slowly up to the platform, there was a hum of noise from in front. I don't recall any profanity or obscenity, although there might have been some. It was just harsh and noisy with the chanting of slogans. As I got up to speak, the noise increased. I just stood there. The noise escalated and continued, and I waited, trying to give them a chance to subside. Finally, one of the students yelled: "Why don't you say something?"

"Well," I said, "I will, if you give me a chance. I'm not about to try to outshout all of you. I haven't got that strong a voice."

Another student said: "That's just the point. You have the chance and we don't."

That was my cue. I said: "All right, I'll make a deal. But it's got to be a deal."

They listened.

"You select someone to come up here. I'll give him ten minutes; I'll listen to him, providing that you give me ten minutes to say what I have to say."

There was an immediate race between two of the boys to get to the platform. Rick Brody (as I later learned) got there first. In all fairness, he was not prepared. When he started to speak, the other part of the audience started to boo him. I got up, motioned them into silence, and said: "Look, we're trying to get a dialogue started here. I wanted a chance to speak, and he ought to have a chance to speak." Somehow I was now in the position of defending his rights, which wasn't bad. Rick spoke and soon said what he had to. It seemed just a few minutes. He did the best he could.

Brody began by saying that this is the chance that students didn't usually get.

"You guys say we are dirty and unwashed. We are the true Americans," he said. They were out on the streets because "no one listened to us in Chicago." He said at one point that he and his fellows were "anti-election." They had no confidence left in politics, and the United States Government, or in the kind of system we had evolved.

When I followed Rick I told of how my father had fled the czarist tyranny of Russian Poland when he was seventeen, to find in America what Rick Brody said they were protesting to find. He had landed here, I pointed out, with only five years of formal education, the ability to work as a tailor, and not much else. One year before he died, his son became the first of Polish ancestry to be elected governor of any state. "Now that may not justify the American system to you," I said, "but it sure did to him." I was trying to say, of course, that if we could do it, they could do it.

I didn't want to belabor them with any argument or try to sell a particular point of view on any single issue. I wanted them to understand that there were those of us within the system who worked and were still working for the objectives that they voiced every day. Maybe we were not as effective as we should be, because of our own weaknesses and faults, and maybe we were not as effective as they would be when they had their opportunity. But I hoped that they would not misjudge the basic good will of the system they criticized, the American idea of making a system responsive to the needs and the voices of more than two hundred million people.

The students' reaction was interesting. They listened and they applauded. When I left the platform, the young people gathered around and they were enthusiastic and cheerful.

It had all turned out well. As for the impact on the campaign itself, apparently the moment got good solid coverage in the evening news. When we reached the Detroit airport, everybody in the crowd seemed to know of the incident in Pennsylvania. They were all fired up. I went to a shopping center rally in which there were some local supporters of Governor George Wallace. I took these hecklers on that afternoon. In that case, I didn't invite them up but I gave them a hard time for the approach they were taking, with their noise and all the rest of it. The rest of the crowd ate it up. Throughout the campaign, I never had the conviction that most of the Wallace hecklers had concerns as legitimate as those of the students. Their only business was disruption. Later in the day at another rally, I invited more students up but they didn't come.

That day Jane had gone on to Denver alone, to make her

first speech in the campaign before an audience of two
thousand United Rubber Workers Union members. Jane
doesn't know what it was, the altitude, something she had
eaten, or the tension, but just before she was called on to
speak she felt a little faint. When they did ask her to talk,
her first words were: "Well . . . I feel as if I'm going
to faint. But before I do, I want to say a word or two about
my husband. . . ."

That little bit of impromptu made a hit, too.

There was a report later that the Students for a Democratic Society had held a meeting as a result of our episode
in Pennsylvania, discussing how they could handle "the
Muskie problem" when I got to Denver.

So we had quite a day.

Perhaps the moment in Washington, Pennsylvania, increased my standing in Washington, D.C., and elsewhere
because, spontaneous as it seemed, there had really been
some preparation for it, at least in the sense that I had
reviewed the options in my mind. The most effective spon-
taneity often has a basis in preparation. If you don't anticipate
and prepare, the chances that you will react intelligently to
events are lessened. I had not specifically planned what
happened, but I had been thinking about what might happen,
I was flexible, and when the cue came I took it.

At first, I must have seemed to the crowd to be angry
at the students' behavior. That brings us, I suppose, to the
subject of my capacity for anger. In various writings about
me there has been a good deal of comment on the fact
that I have a temper. As a matter of fact, I may be responsible for whatever interest there has been in this not very
extraordinary subject. After the 1968 campaign was over,
where the "image" projected had been one of a cool, calm,

unemotional Yankee, I was asked in an interview if I had any weaknesses. I said: "Yes, I do, of course, I do." When pressed further for an inventory, I said that, among other things, I do have a temper. I don't know of many human beings who don't get angry. My father had a pretty good temper and I have one too. He always emphasized to me that the important thing was to learn to discipline yourself, and with his sometimes physical assistance I gradually learned how to do it. I get irritated about little things, but I try not to blow my stack about important things. Perhaps a suitable test of a man is whether or not he displays his temper over little things and keeps his head about the big ones.

At the same time, I think that one ought to be capable of anger about larger matters. If you cannot get indignant about injustice or repression, there's something wrong with you. I'm capable of anger, and of love, of pettiness, of sympathy, and understanding, and misunderstandings. I am, after all, not an iceberg, but a human being; in fact, I suspect that I have the whole range of human emotions. The question is whether or not one keeps these emotions in hand and is emotional about the right things at the right time in the right way. One couldn't go through the kind of campaign we did in 1968 and come out of it with a reputation for being cool and collected without having some capacity for self-discipline.

Another question that arose first in 1968 and continues to this writing is about where I stand. There is a considerable composite body of information available on where any senator stands. I have cast about three thousand votes in the Senate. Those votes should afford a few clues as to how I stand on the important issues of the last twelve years. There is a great body of information available on what I feel deeply about, what I've worked at, what I know about problems, and how I voted on solutions. But it takes homework on the part of those observers who don't know the record.

One thing that amuses me—when it doesn't get me angry —is the question of my "liberal" credentials. My record is apparently a good deal more liberal than people think. It suggests willingness to get out ahead of the pack. In 1970, a mailing put out by a Republican source sought to unveil me as an ultraliberal. I first heard about it at a reception in Cleveland. The host had about one hundred and fifty guests there, representing a wide spectrum of viewpoints, and one couple he identified to me as "McCarthy people" came up. I remember the wife showing me a letter and saying, "I didn't realize you were an ultraliberal." She seemed to derive such happiness from it. I said: "What have you got there?" Then I saw the Republican letter, which concluded that I was ultraliberal because there were two ratings, one from Americans for Constitutional Action, and the other from Americans for Democratic Action. The ACA rating was presumably the test of conservatism while the ADA's the test of liberalism. The ADA ranking showed that I had a score of about 94, compared with something under 90 for Senators Javits, Goodell, McGovern, Kennedy, and others. I was held to be much more liberal than any of these well-known liberals. What the letter writer overlooked, of course, was that while the ACA gave us all a low rating, I was considered more conservative than any of the other "liberals" mentioned.

There is, nevertheless, despite the availability of records, a legitimate point in that anyone who seeks the vice-presidency or the presidency should spell out something more than his basic philosophy. He must actually develop proposals, policies, and programs to deal with current and future issues, as far as one can anticipate. That is part of what a campaign is all about. And as I write this, I expect to go on doing so.

The problem is: How do you present your ideas in a way that answers the questions that people ask? If I could go on television once a week to discuss the issues of the day in depth for all those who care to tune in, I would be happy to do it. It wouldn't be long before we would cover them all. But you make a speech here, and you make a speech there, and it doesn't matter how important or profound it is, most newspaper and television coverage will be made up of the best, or at least the loudest, half-dozen sentences. The papers and the media don't, and perhaps can't, present any comprehensive view of a complex subject or of one's proposals for dealing with it. It is difficult for anyone other than the President to have the opportunity to give people a series of comprehensive statements.

For example, as I work on this section of the book (in early 1972) there is probably no issue on which I have spoken out more or at greater length than on Vietnam. For almost two years I have been clear and unqualified in my support of a deadline for withdrawal. And yet I still run into people who ask: "What is your stand on the war? What is your stand on the deadline?" Even columnists have written this, although the record is clear and by now of considerable length. Communicating and getting across is a problem, and it is all wrapped up in the question of organization, style, staff, money, as well as the courting of the press, the creation of speeches for maximum coverage, and all of the facets of a campaign. I try to get my views before the people, so that they in turn can know where I stand, not just where I'd like to sit. And, imperfect or not, it is very important. I've always regarded this as the heart of politics. I have never regarded political success or candidates as important, except as they relate to ideas that are important, ideas which are responsive to the needs of our country and our people. That is the object of it all.

If we have been successful in Maine, and we have been for over sixteen years, it is because we have concentrated on this aspect of the political process from the beginning. Even before we Democrats had candidates in 1954, we solicited ideas and produced a platform that was regarded as an outstanding example of its kind at the time. My preoccupation with ideas as the center of the political process is as old as my involvement in the politics of one state, and I shall continue to be preoccupied with it.

As the campaign went on, the Vice-President and I did not manage to get together often. One of the key times turned out to be a joint appearance we made on a half-hour television program. Mr. Humphrey and I met at the studio where a dual taping was set up. Groups of people were brought in to ask questions, in an informal atmosphere. It was our one major joint appearance until the eve of the election itself.

The tape was made of the discussion between the studio audience and us, with the material to be used later. Afterward, Hubert and I were just left sitting together. We began to talk between ourselves about the campaign, about the sort of issues and problems that faced our country. It was a spontaneous conversation; it had no construction or outline, but that dialogue—for, unknown to us, the television crew went on taping—may have proved to be our most effective and successful television program. I learned later that, with the exception of a short segment taken out to meet the time requirement, not a bit of editing was done. That program revealed, in addition to our opinions, the rapport between the two of us.

It was said, later, that the campaign we conducted did not have a theme, that there was a race but no central idea. The theme I began to use early, because I felt it, was one of trust, of confidence. I used the same theme for my Election Eve speech in 1970, when I responded to President Nixon's attack on Democrats, because of the sad fact that there had been no diminishing of the need. Apparently, that appeal had an impact in 1968, as in 1970. But it didn't have much visibility, at least on television, because we didn't have enough money to use television early and often enough to make it effective. In addition, ours was not a well-organized campaign. We weren't organized on issues, on themes, on media programs. It was, despite the fact that we started at a low point and ended a good deal further up, a poorly organized, poorly financed, and somewhat demoralized campaign.

The reason for the state of our morale much of the time was largely the Chicago convention and the turbulence that had accompanied it. We didn't believe that we were enemies of the young, strong arms behind a police state, or at odds with all ideals. But that convention left the party and our spirits in disarray. Democrats had also suffered through the abrasiveness of the primaries and, with all Americans, the tragic deaths of Robert Kennedy and Martin Luther King. The divisions within the party on war policy, the talk of a "dump-Johnson" movement, all the fighting in Vietnam and in the streets and parks of Chicago badly fragmented us going into the campaign and exacerbated our problems during much of it.

The task often appeared to be too much. We were preoccupied with trying to get real visibility despite our lack of

money and we had none of the advantages that an incumbent President usually enjoys. We tried to pull together
all elements of the party, including those who had been
alienated and were sitting on their hands. It was difficult,
then, to develop cohesive themes and smooth organization.

The Vice-President and I talked, once or twice, about the
problems and pressures. He had money problems, staff problems, political and diplomatic problems. He was discouraged
in the beginning about getting anybody to do anything. He
was beset, particularly from the McCarthy groups, to attack
or separate himself from President Johnson in return for
promises of support. He was seeking ways to make himself
an independent candidate, to be his own man, without being disloyal. He was often discouraged by the apparent attitude of the President. His problems with President Johnson
may have been more of a lack of communication than of direct heat put on him, as many suspected. The Vice-President
ran for the office of President in full consciousness that the
President was going to react one way or another, to everything he had to say. On September 8, he said that American
troops could be withdrawn from Vietnam in late 1968 or
early 1969. President Johnson, the next day, said: "We
yearn for the day when our men can come home . . . no man
can predict when that day will come . . ." It must have been
an extraordinarily uncomfortable situation. I met with the
President just twice, I think, in the course of the campaign
and he was perfectly friendly and co-operative in tone. But
the tensions for Hubert were something else. He ran, for
one thing, knowing that the peace negotiations were going
on. This was at a time when the world had reason to hope
for more from Paris than we ultimately learned to expect. It
was clear to us, some weeks before the election, that there
might be a cessation in the bombing of North Vietnam and

some movement in the negotiations. That development, which took place only a week before the election, could have broken earlier, except for a speech by McGeorge Bundy at DePauw University on October 12, 1968. The talk, which Bundy said was in no way meant to be partisan, reportedly caused the date for the bombing halt to be set back. All this must have been intensely frustrating for Hubert. He must have known before I did that there was such a peace possibility, that those talks were going on, that a break in the hostilities might occur, and that time was slipping by. Running a limited political campaign is no more advantageous than conducting a limited war. Had the break come earlier, it might have been helpful to us.

What bothered my running mate, I think, was not so much the possibility of Lyndon Johnson's anger or retaliation as it was the feeling that any abandonment of him by the Vice-President would have been hypocritical. This troubled Hubert deeply. He had accepted the responsibilities of being part of the Administration and had defended its policies for a long time. "How *can* I," he would say, "for my own personal advantage turn on him now?" Hubert believed that this would destroy his credibility, but most important, it would have done things to him, deep inside. I don't think that he would have had a problem in adopting war policies that were designed to end our involvement in Vietnam.

At such times, during these candid conversations, I was struck with the difference between the image of Hubert Humphrey, the stump speaker, and Hubert Humphrey, the man talking directly to you about things on which he felt deeply and on which he was as strong as a rock. The Humphrey of those situations is not the glib, rapid-fire speechifier known to much of the public.

We had between us during that campaign a sort of unspoken communication, especially about what I should be doing. He had an instinctive knowledge that we could work well together and work well apart.

From time to time, in the interval since that campaign of '68, I have thought of what might have happened if we had been elected. Whatever may have happened in the primaries of 1972, between the time I write this and the time the book is published, I must say that I think he would have been a very good President. He always had the right qualities and I think they might well have suited the country at that time. This was despite the alienation of many who once supported him and felt that he had left them because of the war. He might never have been able to reassure or win them back, but I think he would have won over enough people to be able to govern. His personal qualities, his warmth, his candor, his quick mind, his ability to understand problems and get to the heart of them, and his imaginativeness in dealing with developing ideas and using them would have been what we needed.

Hubert's major campaign shortcoming was that he somehow never found a way to use television. I can't believe that he would not have found a way eventually, as President, but he never did as a campaigner, despite the fact that he is so articulate and so warm. He was too "big," too "hot," for television, and there was in his style the strong strain of the evangelist, almost a shouter—effective in some crowds, and all wrong for the medium of television.

With his long record in the field of human and civil rights, in compassionate domestic legislation, with his genuine concern, I believed that he would have communicated with people and would have been a good President.

His role for me? Who is to say? He said once that he wanted me as a close adviser—but whether or not that relationship would have materialized remains a question. The President's time is in short supply. It is certainly one of the reasons why he wanted me as his Vice-President. He indicated clearly, for example, that he would turn over to me responsibilities in connection with the cities. I'm sure he would have tried to do that. I am less sure that a President can or should turn over his real or final authority. The President always reserves the final word.

The one major question about Hubert as President was whether he could overcome the fissures that had riven our party and nation because of the war. There was no way of predicting whether he could and no way of second-guessing now whether he might have done it better.

There were other things I would have liked to have done in the campaign, or done better. I would have spent more time in the South, and more time in the border states, especially. I would have liked to have gone back to Missouri—we didn't lose Missouri by much. I wished I had spent more time in Illinois, especially southern Illinois. I wished that my running mate had been able to find a way to deal effectively with his hecklers, or perhaps that was impossible for him, given the size of the task and the fierce energy released against him. I was fresh, new, and unknown, not carrying the burdens that Hubert was. He was the center of their displeasure, and it may very well be that the solution that worked for me would not have been a solution for him at all.

But, all in all, I found it an exhilarating experience. For the first time in my political life, I didn't have to strive for attention. I could be myself and still get attention. It had a liberating effect on me. I could say exactly what I wanted to say, in my own way, and after Washington, Pennsylvania, I didn't have to reach for headlines. I got the coverage, because

nothing succeeds like success. When you have had some
small success, whatever you say becomes wisdom. What the
reporters had been bored with before they apparently decided
must make some sense—because it worked. We built up
what they call momentum. It added tone and excitement to
the campaign, even energy. We ran for office, which means
we really ran. In the last eight days, our schedule had us in
eighteen states. We went from Coast to Coast and from
North to South. In spite of the blur that one's country becomes, you are impressed with a basic unity. You can't be
switching gears to talk differently to one group and then to
another, to have a different message for one interest and then
cater to another in an opposite fashion. You find Americans
sharing values to an amazing extent, responding to the same
basic messages with an amazing similarity. Certainly you
take into account their economic circumstances, whether you
are in agricultural country or in an industrial area, or in the
city, or suburb. But you are really dealing with *people*, not
with types, or lobbies, or special interests. Traveling through
the country at that pace is like driving through the countryside past a stake fence: At the right speed you don't even see
the individual stakes. But you can feel the momentum, from
crowd to crowd, all day long, from early morning until
midnight. It began to feel the same in different states, the
same response, growing crowds at the airport, people staying
later at night, reaching out. There was a rising feeling that
we detected before the polls. The sensitivity to this, when it's
working, precedes the polls. It takes days for the poll results
to be published—and polls are more effective in a state
campaign than in a national campaign, anyhow. There was
a clue out there and it affected us. I'm sure that Hubert
felt it at the same time. The polls were keeping pace with it,
and we began to get the feeling that the election was really
going to work out.

As I went back into Texas, traveling across the Panhandle, into six or seven of the cities, Abilene, Lubbock, Wichita Falls, many of them "Republican" cities, the enthusiasm was astounding by comparison with the first week of the campaign in San Antonio. Now the congressmen turned out, and you knew that some of them wouldn't be there unless they felt that their people were interested. Our meeting in Lubbock was in the middle of the afternoon, a beautiful afternoon of sunshine, with several thousand people in the fieldhouse at the university there. We had high school bands . . . all kinds of music, with dignitaries and dignity. It was the same from town to town, the name of the town didn't matter. In Tyler, Texas, I had a breakfast meeting at eight o'clock, and two thousand enthusiastic Democrats turned out to cheer—Black and white, in East Texas. Fifty-eight thousand people were at a party rally for Hubert in the Astrodome in Houston. And from there to Los Angeles. Our campaign was to end in New England, in Maine, but the Humphrey people had decided on a television show in California and so we struck out for the coast, flying all day. First, there was a rally in downtown Los Angeles—half a million people on the streets, jamming them so that the cars couldn't move, reaching up to pull us off. We began to have enough confidence even to talk about how to form an administration. There were two television programs on Election Eve, one for Mr. Nixon and Governor Agnew, the other for Hubert Humphrey and me, and from all the reactions we heard, we had come out ahead. We were light and at ease, even folksy, I suppose. The Republican program offered Mr. Nixon being asked questions by an interrogator. By comparison, we thought that it was not especially effective.

That last week was a very good week indeed. It fired us

up, and I left the studio and got on the plane and we flew
all night to Maine. We wanted to be at home the next day,
to vote and to rest.

And the rest is history.

There was a theory that if the campaign had gone on for
another week or two, we would have won. You couldn't
help but subscribe to it if you felt the swing of that last week.
It is also possible that we had escalated to our peak.

We had come a long way. In the early stages of the campaign, the Vice-President had been, to a considerable extent,
abandoned by the party regulars. There were local politicians
who didn't know whether they wanted to come and take the
risk of being seen with him or not. There was less of this in
my case, possibly because I wasn't so "tainted." But even
with me there was a marked lack of enthusiasm. Some of
them went through the motions. You could see that they
were doing it without real conviction. You knew how
things were going to work out for you if they continued in
that way. It was amusing later to see the enthusiasm, and
how eager others became to sit on the same platform and
to have pictures taken with you. A candidate and the people
react together, without the intervention of the party regulars;
we really do something to each other—and therefore eventually to the party itself. There is a great fear in this country
of the pols, of political machinery in smoky back rooms. But
there is something going on between the people and the
candidates which transcends this. The television tube is one
of the big intermediaries today. Everyone recognizes its importance, some to the point of asking what is the point of
stirring up things around the country and going through
impossible schedules? There are reasons, such as that one
makes the other more exciting. If a candidate campaigned

just from a studio, it would be a very dull performance, no matter how skillful he was. How could you simulate Washington, Pennsylvania, in a studio, for example? A candidate has to be newsworthy as well as ideaworthy and you do this by traveling around the country. People want to see candidates in person, reacting with people.

Another factor is that television is, chiefly, one-way communication. You have to have two-way talk in order to make the political process meaningful. And so you have to get out, even though it is perfectly true that not many citizens actually have an opportunity to discuss the issues with the candidate himself. But the candidate gets their response to what he's saying in a direct way.

You get that important response directly from audiences, if you are sensitive at all to them. I am sensitive not just to applause, but to the feel of an audience, whether it's good, whether it's bad, whether it's thoughtful, or whether it isn't. You get the comments afterward; they aren't exhaustive but they are representative, and you get the evaluation of the local press. When people come up afterward, if they're not coming up just to get an autograph, but to thank you for saying something in particular, or to appreciate a comment, then you know you have made an impact. I read faces in the crowd. Sounds are less significant, although silence is significant. But above it all is a feeling in the air, especially if it's a thoughtful audience.

When we flew back to Maine, we arrived in Portland at six or seven on Election Morning, drove up to Waterville, and went directly to my old ward to vote. In Ward Seven, there were the same faces who had been there most of my political life, old friends, poll and party workers. They seemed to have been there for years, in that schoolhouse (most voting places in Waterville are schoolhouses, with the one exception of the City Hall), and so it was a true homecoming.

We went to the motel, cleaned up, and had a bite to eat. At noon I went out to play golf and, perhaps symbolically, played well on the first hole and the last hole. That's where the cameras were. In between, I did badly.

The networks had not been particularly pleased that we had decided to spend the evening in Waterville because the location does not offer convenient TV facilities. But I was determined to be there: that's where I had been for every election. We and the press took over the Armory and all the motels—not a bad economic boom for a few days in the old town. Families and friends came down for dinner that evening and we did appropriate justice to Maine lobsters. One of the photographers, Burt Berinsky, who had followed us through the campaign, had put together a show of his excellent slides. The members of the press who had been with me gave me a plaque, commemorating a story I had told many times in the campaign. It became *the* campaign story, I suppose, the one about a Texas rancher who was touring in Maine. He thought that while he was there he ought to have a chance to compare Texas ranching with Maine farming. When he came to an attractive little farmhouse, he stopped and introduced himself and struck up a conversation with the farmer. In the course of it, he said, "By the way, just how big is your farm?"

"Well," the farmer said, "it isn't very big. You can see just about all of it from where we are standing. It begins about down there by that brook and follows the brook to that little tree and then along the fence over to the woods, then the line of the woods to the road, and back here."

"Oh," the Texan said, "that isn't very big, is it? You

know, down on my ranch, if I were to get up in the morning, get into my car at 7 A.M., and travel all day as fast as the car would go, by sunset I might just reach the other end of my ranch."

There was silence.

Then the Texan said, "What do you think of that?"

"Well," said the farmer, "I had a car like that once myself."

I had used the story over and over again, because it was a good one, and unfailing. The press got to wincing but waiting for the punch line, to check the crowds' reactions. So they asked me to tell it for one last time at the rally in Maine. The plaque they gave me has on it an old antique car, and underneath, the line *I had a car like that once myself.*

We didn't watch the returns but we got reports on how they were going, which became less and less encouraging. About eleven o'clock, we went over to the Armory to talk with the crowd there. There was quite a crowd of young people in the place—and they started me off. "What about Chicago?" So I launched into a talk with them, and it was a good, warm, homey kind of meeting. I didn't bother to go back to the Armory later. The results were neither clear nor final, but by the time we got back to the motel, it seemed evident that we didn't have a chance of winning, although at that point it was still not clear that Mr. Nixon would have a clear majority in the Electoral College. So we stayed up until two or three, and then went to bed.

When we got up in the morning, it was pretty much over. So I went out and played golf again. My game was terrible. It was a cooler day. The weather matched my mood.

It had been, for me, a great experience. The letdown I felt was principally for Hubert.

I had thought highly of him at the start of the campaign and I did at the end. We never had a briefing session on the

issues, what he was going to cover or what I would. He left
me on my own. Except for the question of itinerary, I don't
think we influenced each other's plans. We talked when we
could at night, or anytime when I could catch up with him
on the phone, to exchange experiences, crowd reactions, and
observations, and for me to get any orders he had. But he
never gave me orders.

I was impressed especially by his generosity. It would have
been easy for him to resent the praise I was getting, as a fresh
face, for him to be jealous with all the talk about the ticket
being upside down. He didn't; as a matter of fact, he took
pride in what was happening. He took to comparing the two
vice-presidential candidates. His generosity of spirit was, I
thought, a reflection of his qualities as a human being, qualities I had always admired and which were re-enforced by the
campaign.

He campaigned, as I've noted, from a very difficult position,
locked into his loyalties to his country, to his President, to his
party, to his own ideas. There was always the question of his
own credibility, especially on the war. He could not have
changed course 180 degrees, even if he had believed it was the
thing to do. He could not, as an honest man, bring himself
to do a complete turnaround on the war, even though he felt
as I thought, that we ought to stop the bombing. And he
would not do so only to enhance his chances of winning.
Such questions posed such difficult moral issues for the Vice-
President that I never tried to press him. The best service I
could perform was to articulate my own view and my own
doubts about our war policy without being so blunt about it
as to put us on a collision course.

When asked during the campaign how my policy or my
ideas compared with President Johnson's policies, or with
Vice-President Humphrey's, my answer always was: "It's up

to you fellows to make the comparisons. It's for me to state my views as well as I can."

When the Vice-President made his Salt Lake City speech I thought it was a responsible and bold attempt to show his flexibility on the issue of the war, of his willingness to move in the direction of a bombing cessation, a speech in which he undertook to indicate what his directions might be without doing violence to the other considerations just mentioned. The people in the anti-war movement said it wasn't clear-cut enough; he didn't go far enough. President Johnson, obviously, from his reaction since 1968, thought it went too far. It appears that from President Johnson's point of view, the speech destroyed Hubert Humphrey's prospects of winning the election. I thought it helped.

After the election, we went with the Humphreys to the Virgin Islands. There, I could see again how Mrs. Humphrey, a wonderful woman, contributes to her husband's life. They complement and supplement each other emotionally and intellectually. My guess is that Muriel Humphrey adds immensely to her husband's stability and peace of mind.

He was thinking of his future, of where he ought to go, of what he might do. I could see him shifting to the future already. And yet he was marvelous company at St. John; the kids with us just flocked to him. Only occasionally would I see him sitting off on the beach alone, and feel that he was tasting regret.

But such moments were rare and didn't dampen his or our spirits, and we all had a beautiful time.

CHAPTER III

●

One Man's Journey

As I look back to my youth and the influences that shaped me, I go down the list of heroes who inspired me. At this point in my life it is difficult to disentangle the comparisons made between me and political leaders of other times from the real heroes of childhood.

The "Lincoln" label some have pinned on me provides a temptation to say that he was my first and constant hero. I can't claim that, although I did admire President Lincoln and I am flattered by the comparison, even though it has nothing to do with philosophy or greatness, or maybe even goodness. It has more to do with height and posture, and, perhaps, style. I suppose we all envision Lincoln as lanky and laconic, slow and deliberate, earthy and cool. We don't see Lincoln in a great towering rage or in sullen petulance; we see him as mournful. He had the capacity for laughter and a fine sense of humor, but I have never seen a picture of him smiling.

When I was a college senior, we were to have speeches at the class-day graduation exercises. One was to be given by a friend, who wasn't much for speeches, and as class president I was to give one, too. I wrote his and adlibbed mine. I don't know whether he or anyone else noticed, but the one I ghosted for him had been ghosted, so to speak, for me: It was patterned after the Gettysburg Address. The subject matter was not as profound but the style was meant to be similar. In any case, each of our speeches was followed by silence, too.

Lincoln was a hero of mine, just as he is for every youngster. Washington and Lincoln were our standard presidential heroes but Lincoln always seemed, somehow, more human. Over the years he has tended to climb into first place in my evaluation of Presidents. All the others are below those two, that's clear.

Lindbergh was one of my heroes, as well. The trans-Atlantic flight attempts went on through the 1920s, as well as several after his, and some of the later ones originated in Maine. There were not many long air strips around for those heavily loaded planes to take off, and Old Orchard Beach in our state was used for several such flights. But Lindbergh was *the* heroic figure. After the murder of his child, I wrote an ode on greatness, celebrity, and glory. As I recall the first lines, they were:

> Of what use are fame and glory
> They are but the empty praise of fickle mobs

The golden heroes of sports loomed large to us, too, and it was a good time for such heroes: Babe Ruth, Bill Tilden,

Paavo Nurmi, Charley Paddock, Bobby Jones, Jack Dempsey. I remember both Tunney-Dempsey fights; all of us kids were for Dempsey. He was the fighter, Tunney "just a boxer." That was our simplified analysis. We liked the fighter.

Amelia Earhart was our heroine, too, although today's Liberation leaders would be less than pleased to know that she was called "Lady Lindbergh."

In politics, Al Smith was hero to both my father and me. And so, of course, was Franklin Roosevelt.

But of all my heroes, the one who looms largest is my father. He was a remarkable man, whose life became a symbol to me of what is best in America.

My father came from Poland. He was born at a time when czarist Russia controlled the country. Poland was occupied territory, subject to the imperial demands of the czar. Young men were required to serve in the "Polish Army," but they were denied the right to teach or to learn Polish history, to preserve Polish culture. His father had decided that his son should leave the country before he reached the age of conscription, which was seventeen, and so he was apprenticed to a tailor. As soon as he learned a trade, he left home and his homeland, with his family's blessing.

The life my father left was not one of brutality, apparently; he was full of warm talk about incidents from his boyhood. But he was not free, and so he emigrated to England and then the United States.

My mother was from a large Polish family in Buffalo. Her brothers worked in the railroad shops and the girls went to work at an early age, too. When my mother and father married, she made it clear to him that she couldn't cook and she couldn't sew; in fact, she couldn't do many of the things that a young married woman was expected to do around the house. My father made it clear to her that she would learn. In fact, he already had boarders staying at his house, so she was going to have to cook for him *and* the paying guests.

In addition to inherited boarders, she had to take care of the babies that began to arrive after a time. Ultimately, there were six of us. We couldn't afford to buy store clothes and so she learned to sew. She became superb in both departments, cooking and sewing. Ma didn't just limit herself to the simple things. She learned to crochet and to lug wood and stoke fires and boil water and put clothes through a wringer. In the winter, she would hang them out to dry on the porch where they became stiff sheets of ice. This kind of life didn't leave many hours for her to spend time with her children, but she managed some of that, too.

We lived across the road from a hill of fir trees. On a certain Sunday afternoon in December, my father would trudge up and over that hill with his ax. "I'm going to get us a Christmas tree," he'd say. He would come back by late afternoon with a beautiful tree and set it up. When lit, those trees of ours would have a hundred candles on them. Now that I think of it, I would never dare to use candles on a Christmas tree, but they were splendid. Christmas was especially jolly because our parents made it into a day of entertainment. They bought us games—and on Christmas Day they would sit around the table with us, playing them. And books! They always bought us books because we all loved to read. For the girls, my mother would sew whole new wardrobes of doll clothes.

There were, to be sure, turkeys and puddings, pies and cakes for Christmas and Easter. The neighbors and their kids were often invited in and so there was a lot of warmth and cheerful tumult.

Christmas or not, we enjoyed playing cards—whist and casino—and my mother always had chocolates as prizes for those who won. Chocolate-covered cherries were the big stakes. Our chocolate gambling went on all day long; we stacked them up beside us like chips.

My father could tell stories, in addition to giving his opinions forcefully, and though we wearied once in a while of his lecturing, we never tired of his stories. He bought one of the first Victrolas in town. I can see it coming in the door now, that big console with the picture of the dog listening to "His Master's Voice." We would sit around evenings cranking it up and listening. We had a lot of Polish records, including one by a Polish soprano. My father used to sit and listen and laugh at that recording. I wondered what was so funny. "Well," he said, "I can't translate it exactly, but she says that some say when they drink coffee they can't sleep, but she says that with her it's different—when she sleeps she can't drink coffee." He thought that was very funny. Perhaps he cleaned it up for me.

He also bought one of the early radios, with wet batteries to power it, and three dials to synchronize. My parents liked listening to a comedy team called Billy Jones and Ernie Hare. I can see my parents both laughing until their stomachs ached.

In due course my father acquired other things. He bought a car, a Chevrolet, one of the first autos in town, and then a Durant. Eventually he bought a Cadillac. The Cadillac was an old one, but he bought it because it was a seven-seater and we needed it.

He bought the house next door because, he said, he wanted to be able to pick his own neighbors. He believed in paying cash. He earned enough to pay for the house and then he repaired it and put it in shape.

In one or another of his cars, we'd go rolling off to a farm outside the town, owned by some Russian friends. It was a great farm and we loved to go out there. We would roll in the hay and pick rhubarb, and in the fall pick corn off the stalks and boil it to eat right there in the fields. In the summertime we went to a lake or pond to swim.

In August, after the first blueberries had arrived on the bushes, my father would take birch off the trees and make baskets for us to use as we picked them.

My father was not averse to a little pharmacopoeia, either. He remembered remedies from the old country. Whenever one of us came down with hives, he would go out into the country, seek out a special kind of tree, cut it down, bring it home, chop up the wood into pieces, and cook it for three or four hours in a big old ice-cream can over a fire. To make it fun while waiting, he would get some potatoes and bake them in the fire. The potatoes were delicious. The medicine he produced was the most obnoxious stuff known to man, thick, brown, and smelly, and it worked.

He once tried to get it patented, to try selling it, but he did not succeed. Lord knows what the Food and Drug Administration might have said, but there never was a patent medicine that worked as well. Although he never managed to market it, he did give it away to people who had heard about it. Most of them lived.

My interest in the environment, in the great outdoors, is part of a rich heritage from a poor family, especially from my father.

My father was raised on a farm. His father managed a nobleman's property and all the children had the run of the farmlands. There were opportunities in Poland to fish, he always told us, and my father created opportunities for me to fish, too. In the summertime he took Wednesday afternoons off, along with the other merchants and shopkeepers in town.

They used to take us fishing on those afternoons. When I got to be nine, ten, or thereabouts, he took me up into the wilderness, fishing for a week with two of his friends and their boys. There were just the six of us, all by ourselves, and we had great times in those woods. Every father ought to spend time like that with his boy—and I haven't done it as much as I should have.

We headed for an area called Four Ponds. We went by caboose on a freight train to a station called The Summit and we took along a week's supply of groceries and clothing. Then it was a four-and-a-half-mile hike uphill. We had to carry all our stuff on our backs. But once there, we found paradise.

There were not many cottages. We stayed in one of them. There was a Long Pond, a Round Pond, a Sabbath Day, and Little Moxie. The latter yielded fat, chubby, colorful trout. Long Pond had bigger fish. Sabbath Day was just as lazy and quiet as its name and there were more mosquitoes there than fish. Round Pond was a beaver pond and the least productive. Still, they all had what we came for. If we wanted fish for breakfast, we would get up ten minutes early and bring them in. We would fish all day, going from one lake to another. The kids would row, the fathers would fish, and when we got tired, the fathers would row and we would go after the trout, which ran to eight or ten pounds.

At night the men would sit around, playing cards and telling tall tales. We ate plain food, baked beans, prunes, and, of course, fish.

Our outdoor activities weren't limited to the woods. We played ball on the road that ran by our house. Like all families, we had an occasional difficulty with our neighbors. Now and then the ball would go over our heads and outstretched hands and into one neighbor's garden. He had a beautiful house, with lovely fields and a fine vegetable garden enclosed by a fence. When the ball sailed over that fence, the old man who owned the property would go off like a skyrocket.

My father never defended us. "Mr. Hemingway doesn't want you to go over there," he would say, and that was it. He had a strong sense of respect for the rights of others—that meant whoever the others were, from the lowliest to the highest. He insisted upon respect for others and for himself, and as a result I don't know of a man in town who was more respected than he was. My father was a tailor, proud of his craft. He was a good one, the best one, and he made clothes for the mill managers and the doctors and other professional people, people with money.

My father wouldn't put up with any foolishness. He never had much formal schooling, but he learned to speak English and he knew how to express himself—forcefully and clearly. During summers when I worked in the shop, I heard smoking-hot arguments, many of them with customers. A man might spend $500 or $1,000 a year with him, but if my father disagreed about politics, war, peace, prices, taxes, or whatever, they had it out. His opinions were worth more to him than his income.

Pa wasn't cranky; he was just intense. I guess he and I were somewhat alike—he had a temper, but for the most part he controlled it. The last time he ever spanked me was when I was seven or eight. He pulled off his belt and used it on me—once an accepted and widespread technique in the prepermissiveness era—but by mistake he used the buckle end. And it hurt. When he discovered his mistake, he put that belt back on and never spanked anybody again for the rest of his life. But he never let us forget that there were fundamental values that we must honor and observe. Our lives were rooted in the obligations of church, family, and country.

I carried with me constant reminders of those obligations. A Catholic custom requires that every child shall be given at least one saint's name. It is often the middle name, sometimes both the given and the middle names. I was awarded two, for good measure; both Edmund and Sixtus were—until I got them—the names of saints.

Why my mother and father chose those, I don't know. Sixtus is a Roman name and it was the name of five popes. Probably the most famous was the one for whom the Sistine Chapel in St. Peter's was named.

Sixtus, blessed or not, was a heavy load for a small child to carry. Like most, I thought my name so odd that I rarely mentioned it, hoped it would not be discovered, and never fully appreciated its grandeur. It might have been useful if my folks had given me some background, because there is reason to be at least a little proud of the name.

If you're a believer in numerology, each of my names has six letters, and the middle one means six. But I was the second, not the sixth child. And so the "six" theory begins to fall apart at that point. However, my youngest son is my namesake and he seems to take pride in the whole handle.

A few writers have suggested that as a boy I was mocked and friendless. I don't know what their sources were, but I had as healthy and happy a childhood and family life as a boy could wish.

High school was a complete change. Until then, my interests had all been outside school and out of doors—fishing, hunting, baseball, football, and skiing in the winter.

One of my biographers has reported that I was an indifferent center on the basketball team, that once when the coach was looking for me to put into the game that I was found off in a corner somewhere, reading a book. That's a pretty episode, I guess, and strikes a blow for literacy, but I don't know where the story came from. I very much wanted to make the team. I was off practicing, as I recall.

I had never played basketball before I got to high school. We were interested instead in sandlot football and baseball. In the winter, our sport was skiing. Rumford was one of the first skiing centers in the East, with one of the first good ski jumps. That was the kind of skiing we did, with the emphasis on jumping, not in downhill or trail skiing. Often, I would ski before breakfast and come back from school and ski by moonlight, I loved it so. But when we got to high school, basketball became engrossing. I tried track and football and gave up skiing, but I had the same problem in all sports: I didn't have stamina. I was acquiring a little too much height too quickly. When I entered high school I was five feet four inches tall and when I left, I was six four, and I hadn't gained weight to go with it. I winded easily and couldn't play in a game very long. I lasted long enough to win a letter in basketball, although as it turned out I was more adept at track.

Without really applying myself, I ran a fair half mile. I had a good stride, and some speed, and won a few races. The meet I remember best is the final one of my senior year.

We had been high jumping in my backyard, just for the fun of it, but it had never occurred to me to try out for that event on the track team. The day before the last dual meet, I wandered over to where the high jumpers were practicing and joined them. I seemed to do as well as they were doing. The next day, I ran in my event, the half mile, and lost, and then went over to the high jump and won the event. Few other events have come that easily for me.

In high school my interests also became more intellectual,

and my friendships changed. We lived in one part of town
which was called Virginia, and the high school was in the
other end. Now I became totally engaged with my courses,
with trying to do well, with marks, and getting into college.
I joined school organizations and held class office. Many of
the kids I had grown up with weren't interested in such
things, and I developed new friends. High school became an
exciting time. That is when I began to fight off the shyness
that had plagued my childhood. I was forced out of it because my interests and my teachers led me out. I had the best
break you can have in school—several inspired teachers. Lou-
ise Hicks, who later became Mrs. Warren, was our American
history teacher. We flocked to her room after school for discussions of current events. In 1932, we nominated Franklin
Roosevelt early, perhaps before he knew he was going to be
the candidate. Miss Celia Clary, now Mrs. Fossett, was our
English teacher and debate coach and she, too, was tops. She
should have been the track coach, because she ran me down,
chased me, caught me. For days I had tried to escape her,
but she thought I was a prospect for the debating team she
was trying to put together. I was glad, eventually, that she
did catch me. But getting up to make my first speech was a
painful experience, for me and the audience.

A big debating issue in those days was the matter of chain
stores. There was considerable resentment against them. In
one debate I was to argue that chain stores didn't give you
as good a measure as independent stores. In preparation for
it, we bought two cans of pears, one from a chain store, one
from an independent, each the same size. We then proceeded to show the similar labels, open them on stage, and
compare the contents. It was to be a dramatic, risky experiment. The can from the independent store was filled to the
brim with pears. The one from the chain store was full, too—

of peaches. We hadn't expected to make our point quite that way, but every little mistake helps.

Meanwhile, I worked with my father. I learned to sew, to do minor alterations on trousers, and to press. I became a good pressman, working with a heavy hand iron. It was in his tailor shop that I learned the most about his political and social views. My father was always talkative, even more so than I became. Three things governed his life: his love of Poland, his intense love of freedom and independence and therefore of this country, and his strong sense of family. He sensed the continuity, the line out of the past and into the generations ahead, generations that he would never see.

I think these qualities were true of a lot of Americans we now call "ethnic groups." They had a sense of what brought them here. And I suspect that not knowing or feeling this is partly responsible for the distance between the generations now alive.

The children and young people who do not feel this sense of continuity with their past don't have the respect for the people who went before them, because they can't see it. They are not without a sense of heritage, and they certainly sense something beyond the immediate present, but they do not always talk about that heritage, as my father did or form their attitudes in direct response to it. Even so, I believe the majority of young people cling fiercely to fundamental values —values that our common heritage has delivered to them, of compassion, tolerance, co-operation. We have taught our children precisely what the immigrants wanted—to be safe, to be respected, to be left alone. These lessons are not re- flected in surfaces: in the clothes they wear, the length of their hair, the vocabulary they invent, or the music they make. They are reflected instead in the traditional American commitment that one generation can somehow *improve* on its predecessors. Neither they nor we have ever destroyed the promise of America.

My father, like a lot of others, came in search of a spirit. De Tocqueville wrote that "America is a land of wonders," and so he and other immigrants came, I think, in search of wonder. They came not as oppressors, but usually as people oppressed. They came not to practice violence, but to live in peace. They came not to colonize, to exploit, or destroy a country but to build one—first a home, then a community, finally a nation. Their work, our work, is not complete. And some people seem to give up on it as a bad job when it is, in reality, an unfinished journey, a partly done job. Perhaps a nation is like a great cathedral, never quite finished, always changing, with more to add, and yet standing there, immense, imposing, and impressive, inviting the contribution of a new generation.

CHAPTER IV

●

Into the Environment

As SOME PEOPLE know, I have long been involved in the issue of environment, so much so that I am working on a separate book about its thorny and complex issues. All that is pertinent here, perhaps, are a few notes on how and when my interest began, without writing vast campaign claims to greatness.

The environment into which I was born had some of heaven about it, but earthly problems were there, too. My land was a place of great natural beauty. It was also a paper mill town where pollution seemed an inevitable, if ugly, reality.

When I was a boy, we didn't think about "pollution." The word wasn't part of our everyday vocabulary, and it was hardly in the public dialogue. If we thought at all of such matters, what we saw appeared to be a necessary balance between jobs and some pollution of a river; between wide, open, clean spaces, streams, lakes, forests, mountains, and a few less than lovely factories or plants. The beauties of nature were around us in almost pristine form. What development we had was the price we paid for the economic benefits, even if it defiled the river some.

Yet it was our river, the Androscoggin, that stirred public concern and indignation even before World War II. The Androscoggin begins its run to the ocean in the high, clear mountain streams and lakes in the northwestern corner of Maine. It flows into New Hampshire, then back into Maine, picking up pulp and paper wastes in Berlin, New Hampshire, Rumford and Livermore Falls-Jay, Maine. In those days, more than thirty years ago, the mill wastes were visible long before the river reached Lewiston. There was a tremendous stench, and the paint on houses began to peel. A court suit resulted in a court order. The river was placed under the jurisdiction of a Bates College chemistry professor, Dr. Walter Lawrance, who was called "The River Master." He worked with the companies, on behalf of the court, to eliminate the public nuisance of the pulp wastes, if not its cause. By the time I was in the legislature in the late '40s and early '50s, there was talk of dealing with the pollution problem. The court order hadn't produced much change on the Androscoggin. The paper companies had spent some money, but it had not been adequate. The legislature enacted a "water improvement" law in 1953 that classified all the waters of the state by the degree of pollution. It was an innocuous beginning. It simply meant identifying the current state of those waters, not doing anything about them. Not that this was necessarily foolish or hypocritical: We had to find out where we were before we tried to recoup.

Even that modest piece of action stirred opposition, and there was nothing like the current widespread concern about pollution. Jobs were important and they came first. The people in the towns that lined the rivers and depended upon industries for jobs and a tax base believed that you shouldn't rock the boat and impose impossible burdens upon their industrial resources. It might upset the economy of the town and affect jobs, taxes, and the ability of communities to pay for schools and other public services. The paper companies were happy to use these arguments in the halls of the legislature and before committees to inhibit and restrain tough legislation. There was no secret about all this; it was a public argument.

The water classification program did not clean up Maine waters, but it gave the illusion of an anti-pollution effort. With the exception of a few conservationists, there were no energetic campaigners for a change in Maine's law.

When I was elected governor, the environment wasn't an issue between the parties. In fact, I don't think that pollution had been a significant issue in any of the state campaigns up to that time. No one was for pollution, but the citizens of Maine were not aroused against it. The Maine Democratic Party platforms of 1954 and 1956 are instructive. In 1954, we called for enactment of an "anti-pollution law, tested by experience elsewhere, together with necessary positive legislation to combat problems of industrial and sewage pollution." In 1956, the year I ran for re-election, our platform recommended "strengthening the present State laws controlling water pollution to prevent any increase in the present level of pollution and to provide a deadline for the start of pollution abatement, with a flexible time limit to prevent unreasonable hardship during clean-up operations in complex cases of contamination." That was hardly a call to the ramparts, but it did signal the move from classification of waters as they were to an effort at water quality improvement.

In 1955 and 1956, I had tried to accelerate the process of classifying the rivers. We had not had a sufficient sense of urgency about that task. I decided to hurry up the job of classifying so that we would know the magnitude of what we had to do. By the spring of 1956, I was ready to make the next move, and federal legislation passed that year gave us the boost we needed. The Congress enacted the first federal program to help communities build waste-treatment plants. I thought we ought to move aggressively on the state level, so in January of 1957, I proposed to the legislature that we create a state program to match the federal grant to build treatment plants. I also suggested that we use the classification work that had been done to begin upgrading the streams—in other words, to set classifications for what ought to be, not just what existed. There was resistance and a fight on the floor of the Maine House. Some streams were eliminated from the proposal, but we established the principle that the classification system should be used to upgrade the quality of the waters.

Each of those programs has been built upon since. The initial programs were so obviously inadequate that they couldn't accomplish much, practically speaking. They did establish principles and precedents.

When I came to the Senate and was assigned to the Public Works Committee, I had some reason to welcome the assignment as well as a little background for it, even though the committee was not one I sought. In 1963, a special Subcommittee on Air and Water Pollution was created by the chairman Senator Pat McNamara. With the creation of the subcommittee, we were really given a forum. We prepared a preliminary staff report, "Steps Toward Clean Water," and wrote the first draft of what became the Water Quality Act of 1965. With the results of staff studies, my own convictions about the need for water quality goals led to a water quality standards section, which was the centerpiece of the Act.

We were able to hold hearings around the country, to stir up public interest, and with a lot of hard work over two years, we got momentum started for the legislation which has developed ever since.

Air pollution was a new field for me when I entered the Senate. In 1957, when Senator Abraham Ribicoff was Governor of Connecticut, he was appointed chairman of a committee at the Governors Conference to delve into the whole question of air quality, especially pollution from automobiles. As Secretary of Health, Education, and Welfare in the early years of the Kennedy administration, he was responsible for the federal government's limited air-pollution-control effort. From where I sat, he was the most visible man in the field— which was not, as I've said, much of a field as yet. I think that the early 1960s were the first time that many people, certainly legislators, began to think of air pollution as controllable. The notion that you could somehow prevent the escape of gases into the atmosphere and yet continue the functions that produced them had been inconceivable, especially with respect to the automobile. Most of us had accepted the idea that if we wanted civilization and its technological wonders air pollution was a by-product, something that went with progress, and not something we could really prevent.

Legislation was initiated in the House in 1963, and when it came to the Senate the bill was referred to our committee. Armed with the House action and our hearing record, we got busy. The air pollution bill produced was the first pollution legislation that we reported out of the subcommittee and it was enacted into law. We have been going on ever since.

If it hadn't been for the question of air pollution, I doubt that there would be the heightened general concern about pollution. You can escape water pollution . . . at least for a time. You cannot escape air pollution.

Many of us live out of sight of water. In our day-to-day requirements for drinking, bathing, cooking, our water, no matter how dirty at the source, is cleaned up enough so that we are not always aware of the purity of the end product, or of the streams which carried it toward us. But air is there to breathe, and in too many cities and towns you can taste it and almost feel its deposits in your lungs.

Air pollution provided much of the momentum for our fight against all forms of pollution. It also provided its share of villains for environmentalists and the general public to attack. The early targets were the smoke emitters—the steel mills, the power plants, and the incinerators. In later years, with growing concern over smog and carbon monoxide, the automobile has become the symbol of our air pollution crisis, and with good reason.

By a coincidence of geography, meteorology, and history, Los Angeles became the early warning signal for automotive pollution in the United States. The great basin between the mountains and the ocean, bathed in the sun of southern California, was a mecca for Americans looking for a chance to better their lot. And Los Angeles grew on the wheels of the automobile, sprawling across the great basin, up the hillsides and through the passes to the valleys beyond. More and more people thronged in during the Depression, the war years, and after; cars stimulated more road construction and more roads attracted more cars. And all the while, the insidious thermal inversions that put an invisible lid over the air in the basin were trapping the automobile exhausts. That combination of unburned hydrocarbons and nitrogen oxides was baked in the basin, forming the haze and acrid gases that came to be known as smog. At first, industry and incinerators were blamed, but in the late 1940s scientists were able to demonstrate that the ubiquitous automobile was the prime offender in destroying the air of Los Angeles. It took more than fifteen years to apply that lesson on a national level.

In 1965, the Subcommittee on Air and Water Pollution moved to apply federal controls to automotive exhausts. California had developed a vigorous state program, but that did not help New York, or Washington, or Chicago, and we were gathering evidence that California's air pollution problem was not unique. We wanted to require compliance with federal standards, because automobiles do not stay in one jurisdiction and because we believed it was a national problem. We soon encountered opposition that became drearily familiar, year after year. Administration witnesses testified in support of our findings that automotive pollution was a serious national problem, but they questioned our proposal to impose deadlines on the industry. The Administration doubted the technological capacity of the automobile manufacturers to achieve the proposed controls within the time limits spelled out in our legislation. The White House had passed the word that it wanted to work out a voluntary agreement with industry.

After we heard the Administration's recommendations, the subcommittee went to Detroit for field hearings and an examination of the manufacturers' research and development facilities. There representatives of the automobile manufacturers testified that they did not believe automotive pollution was a national problem, but that if the Congress insisted on the deadline contained in the Senate bill, the manufacturers had the capacity to meet it. On our return to Washington we invited the Administration spokesman to make a return appearance before the subcommittee. He "clarified" his earlier testimony and said that the industry's reaction had removed the Administration's basic concerns over the proposed limitations on automotive exhausts. Since that breakthrough, the Congress has tightened the limits on individual vehicle emissions, culminating in the 1970 Clean Air Act that set strict requirements for certification and compliance with legislatively set standards by 1975. We are hearing the same old complaints that the problem is not as serious as we have claimed and that the cost of compliance may ruin the industry. Congressional estimates of pollution dangers have not been 100 per cent accurate, but I cannot remember a single instance where our subcommittee has overestimated the pollution threat. If we have learned anything about the threats to health and welfare from exhaust emissions, it is that we have underestimated their damage to life and property.

It would be easy to brush aside industry complaints about the latest automotive requirements. Industry spokesmen have cried "wolf" so often, I am skeptical of their alarums and excursions. I know also that they have not been inclined to move until they have been nudged and sometimes shoved. We do know, however, that we are approaching the outer limits of possible restrictions on emissions from the internal combustion engine, and as yet we have no convincing evidence that the industry is ready to make any major shifts to other types of engines. For these reasons there are growing demands to restrict the flow of automobile traffic in our major cities, because we know that the growth in automobile traffic has limited the impact of our real gains in reducing engine emissions.

It is easy, almost too easy, to decree that the automobile

must be removed as the principal source of urban air pollution. To decide what to do about it is not so easy, especially since we have failed to construct adequate public transportation systems that offer an alternative. And until we are willing to provide alternative forms of transportation, it is unrealistic to talk about drastically limiting the role of the automobile. That kind of decision must trigger others, affecting living and working patterns within our metropolitan areas. It will determine allocations of capital, away from highways and to mass transit systems. It will affect our freedom to go where we want to, when we want to, in our own private vehicles. But that limitation on our freedom may be essential if we are to preserve the freedom of all men and women to draw a breath of clean air, and to live.

It is happening now, even if slowly. Mayor John Lindsay closed off Central Park to auto traffic on weekends. He limited parking in the tight canyons of Wall Street and other business sections of Manhattan. Such measures help, but it would have helped even more if, years ago, the height of buildings had been limited. Two new giant towers in lower mid-Manhattan promise to increase traffic, increase the density of people in an area, increase pollution. In Washington and London, there are limits to building size, and thus to population density in them. We have to get further into the questions of open space, population densities, public transit, zoning, the location of industry, all of the activities and factors that affect pollution. All have to be considered in an over-all, integrated plan if we are to be able to breathe other than poisoned air.

The notion that one source of pollution is the enemy is neither accurate nor fair, tempting as it is to point at the automobile, or the power plant, or the steel mill. Eventually, environmentalists get to bucking environmentalists. City lovers want new power plants built out of town. Those out of town don't want their view or their rivers spoiled. We are reaching a point where the power companies, in spite of our growing demands for energy, are not able to find any place to locate new plants. In spite of our demands for oil (not just the oil companies' desire to sell oil), no one wants a refinery around. In spite of our need for desulphurized fuel, we aren't able to build a desulphurizing plant anywhere. One refinery, the subject of controversy in Maine, was to be located on an island in Penobscot Bay. It was a desulphurizing plant. We have to have such plants if we're to have cleaner air in cities, but Maine people didn't want one to clutter up their environment. We encounter a similar conflict in the problem of sludge from waste-treatment plants being dumped into the ocean, reducing one kind of water pollution and increasing another.

One author, William Bronson, has written that it will probably take a massive human kill to bring about the necessary strict regulation against air pollution. There have been kills, in London, in New York, but the analyses of causes are after the fact and dryly statistical. When an airplane crashes and lives are snuffed out, one feels the pain and understands the problem of congested airways. But when congested air produces death by pollution, the fatalities are not easily visible. A statistical study of the death rate in a city during a period of bad air pollution does not have the same dramatic impact as a crash. Slow death is not such good "copy," doesn't stir us as readily. Yet one of the chronic effects of bad air is death.

The rising level of public concern, I believe, does support tough legislation. Perfect legislative solutions are not handily come by. Yet the fact that we could impose a deadline on automobile manufacturers, the fact that we can "interfere" with the long love affair of the American with the automobile is an indication of what we can do.

There is growing evidence that what we think we can do is not enough. The recent study sponsored by The Club of Rome as part of its project on the predicament of mankind* gives a sobering picture of what can happen if we continue to pursue the illusion that growth is the automatic solution for our social and economic problems. Our natural resources are finite, and our reserves of some of them can be measured in decades. Important industrial metals such as chromium, fossil fuels, and arable land will not support unlimited population growth or, more importantly, present trends in per capita consumption. And that reduction in available natural resources is overshadowed by the spreading destruction of land and water by the accumulation of our wastes.

It is hard for Americans to get used to the idea that there is no limit to what we can do or what we can find, if we put our minds to it. Europe was crowded, saddled with conflict and poverty and the dead hand of the past, but our ancestors explored and exploited a new wilderness. When eastern cities, farmlands, and forests seemed inadequate to our needs, there were fresh lands to the west, waiting only for our ingenuity and energy. (And to our shame, we paid little heed to the American Indians and their land that we took over to exploit.) In recent years we have found new sources of petroleum and other materials beyond our shores, the property of underdeveloped nations eager to sell to the industrial nations. But now we are finding that the new sources are running out, and those who control the dwindling supply of resources are demanding higher prices. It is all part of a spreading economy of scarcity.

* Meadows, Donella H., *et al.*, *The Limits to Growth*, New York, Universe Books, 1972.

Even those resources we regarded as renewable are not immune. Whales, haddock, and Pacific salmon species are threatened by overfishing. Species that breed in estuarine waters are being injured by land fill, municipal and industrial wastes, and hot water discharges from power plants. There is a "dead sea" off the mouth of the Hudson River, the product of years of dumping that was not supposed to cause us any problems. Lake Erie is virtually dead, as are thousands of other lesser lakes overloaded with nutrients and the by-products of the good life. The delicate web of life is threatened by our desire to acquire, to use, and to move on to something newer, bigger, and better.

There is reason to take heart, however. Despite the magnitude of our job, I suspect that there has never been any time in the earlier history of man when this fact was seen. In decades and ages past, it was master the wind, conquer the land, and tame the oceans. Now we know that we will have defeated ourselves if we overpower the total environment.

A certain amount of material waste is built into our present society. John Kouwenhoven, in *The Beer Can by the Highway*,† wrote that the shiny metal objects we see reflected back in the headlights of our cars deface the landscape and are also a symbol of our affluence, of our *ability* to waste, and, perhaps, of our need to do so. You cannot have abundance without waste. If every object was built with as much quality as possible, it would be heavier, more expensive, and last so long that we would need less production, meaning fewer man hours, fewer men at work, and lower wages. Much of our Gross National Product is truly gross. We are making products which for both buyer and seller will lose

† Kouwenhoven, John, *The Beer Can by the Highway*, Garden City, New York, Doubleday & Company, Inc., 1961.

their usefulness in a relatively short time, although the payments may last longer than the product.

My father never bought anything on credit. He believed, along with many others of his generation, in paying cash. Not too long ago my mother hauled out the bill of sale on their household goods. She found the papers somewhere listing all the furniture he bought, the dishes, blankets, sheets, and towels. These cost something like $300 and he paid cash. Because he paid on the line, he got a clock that I now have, a chiming clock that sits on our mantelpiece at the beach, reminding me of a time when men settled their debts on the spot.

I admire my father for the principle, but the times changed and so did the rules of the game. What would happen if all Americans had practiced that theory of economics? The Gross National Product would be some minor fraction of what it is. The dollar would be worth more, necessitating less manipulation by the Administration, perhaps, but there would surely be fewer of them and prices, while more stable, would be higher. I am not sure what would have become of our standard of living, that is, for those of us who think we have a standard worth preserving.

And to speak of such standards reminds me of another separation between the generations. The clothes worn by some of the young, the kind of simple life they prefer, their reliance on a few blankets and a lot of hair, signal the fact that to them our standard of living may represent poverty— poverty of the spirit. In any case, our standard of living is mainly material, not spiritual, and in order to enhance it we have elaborated the credit system. If we could (I'm not saying that we should) shorten product life even more, we would have a greater Gross National Product, even if some of the individual products were less than wonderful. I noted last fall that some European manufacturers have been talking about a disposable car, to be driven a few thousand miles and then discarded. That carries the annual model change to its extreme. We have agreed, whether we know it or not, to go along with obsolescence, accepting the satisfaction of style. Some waste is understandable and some may even be desirable. But we are learning, even as we seek to expand the prospects for some of our citizens, that more and more does not necessarily add up to twice as much. In the architectural maxim, sometimes less is more. Every American statistic that I remember, the population of my home town, or the size of the school, or the weekly paycheck, or the Gross National Product, all the statistics which we were taught had most meaning if they were going up. We continue to think this way. But what else do those cheerful statistics mean? They mean that we are running through our resources at too fast a clip. They mean that we are trying for more of everything. That, I guess, is part of what many kids are resisting—the false standard. How far is up?

Some cities still fight for the old-fashioned distinction of becoming larger. Others, large enough, are losing population —and frequently losing part of a populace that could help make them better places to live. Wages are "up." We hear of 30 per cent wage settlements, 30 per cent over three years. I doubt if many people are fooled by that sort of announcement. I can't believe that anyone who is a party to such contracts believes that at the end of three years, after that 30 per cent increase has gone into effect, that in real terms there will have been much improvement. A 30 per cent increase becomes a device to keep even. And that phenomenon, in which staying even becomes such a frantic goal, is a comment on our values, our economy, the direction we call up. Some of our young critics are right, although they are not alone: We would be well advised to question this direction; we would be well advised to ask ourselves what we most want to do with our resources and our lives.

The obvious and simple answer to the dangers of environmental collapse would be to restrict growth and to halt pollution, but to take these steps without counting the human costs would be as great a wrong as to continue the heedless exploitation of the planet. If we really care about the hopes and aspirations of men and women, especially those whose opportunities have been limited, we cannot with callous indifference destroy livelihoods by closing polluting mills, unless we are prepared to make good on the social and economic costs to those who depended on such mills for employment. We cannot by fiat end the quest for economic growth unless we are prepared to deal with questions of distribution of income and services, of making sure that the quest for environmental quality is not simply another instance where the poor pay the burden for others' comforts. This is not only humane, it is the only realistic course, if we are not to endure worse strife than we have known, at home and overseas.

These are not pleasant prospects, and we sometimes weary of the tales from the doomsayers, but I believe that we must consider these prospects and, if possible, act on them. Eventually, dramatic and apocalyptic environmental rhetoric could lose its force and credibility through repetition. I have thought as much on more than one occasion when sitting through a hearing or on a platform. No matter, there will remain the need to carry on with the dull, undramatic, frustrating task of finding the techniques to do the job. The need for compassion, concern, outrage are all there and will remain, too, but we will have to go beyond rhetoric, beyond the fashionable aspects of the issue. It was not fashionable when I first got involved and it may not be again. The tendency to seek simplistic solutions has to be avoided. The objective I sought on automobiles is, in a sense, simplistic, but I took that step because the automobile is not only a polluter but a very important symbol. It was significant to do something that direct and that difficult if we were to help people understand the breadth of the problem, the depth of our commitment, and the prospect that things can be done.

The counterattack has been mounted. *Life* magazine was persuaded that the automobile legislation is unrealistic and impractical. The advertisements of the automobile companies on television are, at the moment, geared to selling their efforts to deal with curing pollution, as if they were doing all that can be done. The Administration has been resisting our efforts to set target dates for cleaning up air and water pollution.

I think that we've written some good legislation. But it has not yet made a sufficient impact. It has, in particular instances, helped considerably; over-all, the problems are worse than they were when we started writing such laws eight years ago. Population growth, the spread of the industrial establishment, increased commercial and personal activity of all kinds affect the several forms of pollution. We have produced pollution at a rate faster than we have moved. Now we are at that stage where it is popular to be for pollution control, for "environmental quality," because so few people to this moment have had to make the hard choices. We have been asked in the past year or so, "Is the environment a political issue?" In one sense it isn't, as things stand, because everybody is for an improved environment one way or another. It is like motherhood or the flag in an earlier day, before those symbols attracted antagonists. But as Barry Commoner wrote in December 1971, environment is not a "Motherhood issue." Nor is it just a local or domestic concern. "Pursued to its source," said Commoner, "every environmental issue generates a confrontation with the grave, unsolved, intensely contested issues of the world—war, poverty, hunger, and racial antagonism."‡

One of the frictions, of course, is that each person perceives other people or institutions as the despoiler. It often appears to be the good guys against the manufacturers (or other polluters). But, as in race or war, the issue is not black or white: The task is to get the antagonists to see another sort of "ecological" balance more clearly; the environmentalist to see that commerce and industry have to live, if we are to live; and for the commercial or industrial man to see that no one will live, work, or profit, including him, if there is not a satisfactory world in which to do so. To see beyond the arguments, beyond the moment, beyond the fiscal year or one's own backyard takes vision, leadership, explanation and education, and courage.

So, to leave off here for the moment, and to inflict my views in another book, I will only return to where I started. My journey toward a place in the environmental sun began in my backyard, in the environment of the place where I was born and raised. There you were, viscerally, an outdoorsman and a conservationist. If you were born in Maine, you got interested in doing something about it when that beauty was threatened. The fact that my state is still writing some of the toughest legislation in the nation is attributable to our desire to preserve the natural wonders of home. There may be no stronger motivation.

‡ New York *Times,* December 7, 1971, p. 47.

CHAPTER V

•

Toward Freedom

We have assumed for two centuries that a free society gives an individual the opportunity to develop, to achieve his or her own potential, to satisfy personal needs, family needs, and those of the community and society. Somehow, that hasn't come to pass.

You can identify the points of failure: All members of our society haven't really been offered the full opportunities of freedom; and apart from all questions of prejudice, discrimination, and the barriers between peoples, we haven't yet produced the ways or the wisdom to make possible the development of an individual's full potential.

For one thing, people must have important goals before they can hope to achieve them. Too many of our children are born into a world where they have no reason to hope for something better than poverty or discrimination.

Child psychologists and educators have told us that what children learn—or do not learn—in the first five years is exceedingly important. Whether or not we accept this theory wholly, we can recognize that a very substantial portion of a child's ability to grow is determined in the early years of life. This is both a frightening and a promising insight. It worries parents who think that they have lost that opportunity with their children who are over the hill at seven or eight or ten. Such fatalism is a natural misunderstanding, a too ready acceptance of the superficial aspects of an important new idea. But the promising side of the same theory offers us a chance to move on several problems of the ghetto, to reduce some of our tasks to manageable proportions. A year or more ago, I began to think that if those first five years are so important, then we have a clearly defined chance to help children, now and in the future, who are born into poverty or discrimination or both. Substantial efforts to give these children a first lease on life could be made—and at tolerable cost. With such an emphasis, we might, in effect, achieve a forty-five-degree turn in the direction of a better society. The potential for building, enriching, liberating young lives excites my imagination. This is the kind of prospect that is emerging now; as we near the two hundredth year of our country's existence, we may be finding the keys to its future.

One welcome station on this journey would surely be equal opportunity, equal access to opportunity for everyone.

The next step would offer the individual the means to take advantage of these opportunities. We have fallen short on both counts, but the pressure to do better is here. It was not intense enough in the past, but now and then we catch glimpses, through the storm of our time, of those stations ahead.

Until we do reach those stations, we will be wasting valua-

ble lives. And that waste will be as monumental as our waste
of resources through careless misuse and the ravages of war.

I think of those first five years of life as an opportunity
to stop the waste of lives. It is also like thinking of going to
the moon: It is an achievable, measurable, objective. You can
"program" it. It may take years but it can be done. If we
think of our population as not just a mass of problems but as
a group of individual possibilities, think of what we can do.
New human beings, just being born, coming into a world
that is prepared for them, wants them, expects them, and, to
an extent unguessed before, knows what to do for them,
would be good news. A true head-start program must be
prenatal, plus the first five years of life. And this would deal
not only with the child but with the mother and the family
and the circumstances in which they live. It is a manageable,
mapable objective and the first glowing signs of it are exciting.

Someone once said to me that he believes in the necessity
of oversimplification; that, for instance, he believes that people have the right to draw a breath of fresh air. He said that it
is oversimplifying, too, but equally intolerable that in a country of our natural and earned wealth, hundreds of thousands, perhaps millions live in poverty while the rest of us
who "fought and clawed our way into the middle class," or
who were born to a degree of affluence, should continue to
"make it" comfortably.

Is that intolerable?

Intolerable, to me, is not the proper testing word. It is
distasteful, even hateful, and at the least undesirable. The
real question is what do we do about it? That brings us, inescapably, to the cherished concept of freedom.

Let us assume a society in which every person is free to
seek and find his or her own level of creativity, attainment,
achievement, or prosperity.

Because abilities vary, individual capacities for achievement vary. Left to chance and our own devices, each of us will attain a different standard of living. If we rely entirely upon natural forces and natural abilities as the measure of what each human being can do with his own life, we will end up with people who get less out of life than humanitarians would hope for. Freedom alone will not do the job. Freedom alone, in the Spartan sense, means that the strong will prevail and the weak take the consequences. This is so-called natural selection.

Freedom, by itself, will not bring the society we seek, if we intend for that society to be not only egalitarian but humanitarian.

In an absolute wilderness there is absolute freedom. If one man inhabits a trackless forest of a hundred thousand square miles, he has reached the ultimate in total theoretical freedom. He is free to go wherever he wants and to do what he wants. His freedom is checked by his own limitations. It is also inhibited by the very immensity of the wilderness in which he finds himself. Both of these are serious limitations but he is, by almost any definition, free.

At the other extreme: In one section of that wilderness add a hundred million people. The demands of the millions upon the resources of their cleared patch of the world constitute the first limitation on all their freedom. To that we must add the multiple demands they impose on each other.

Neither extreme represents genuine freedom: The unleashing of opportunity for the individual spirit to develop, to grow in understanding and ability, to decide for oneself what sort of life he or she wants to live. In each case, survival is paramount. Beyond that, establishing priorities becomes difficult and soon calls for compromise.

What is freedom? As we look back, it is rather easy to understand what the founding fathers seemed to have in mind. Freedom in 1776 was a definition self-imposed on a country of less than three million people—that is, if you count, as they did, whites only. Theirs was, over all, a splendid concept of freedom in contrast to its European paternity. The young nation was by and large uncrowded, immature, not fixed by any particular economic or social formula.

It was, as we have learned to say to others, underdeveloped. It was in many respects freer than the society we have made, because it was less restricted by class or economic distinctions, although it was certainly not without them. When we try to transfer their conception of freedom to our own time—and I mean not just their words but their application to our environments and realities—we are hard pressed. The continentals who congressed still make immense and immaculate sense in the larger abstractions of their thought, but we cannot reproduce the Philadelphia of 1776 in the Philadelphia or Chicago or the Harlem or Watts of 1972.

Freedom is a flexible and a changing concept. Even from such a perspective, we have a long way to go. The art is to balance the understandable desire of the individual to decide his own course and develop his talents against the needs and desires of whatever number of human beings happen to occupy the same cleared space in the forest, the same planet, as he does. This fact tends to put limits on his freedom, restrictions on his possibilities.

Freedom is a bustling, busy concept, not a fine, fixed word chiseled in granite, bronzed on a plaque, or safely sealed under museum glass. It is one of those words we all use, assuming that others, in our own country at least and in most of Western Europe, will understand. And yet few people agree on what it means and fewer still think that its meaning must constantly change and evolve.

The development of this country, like that of England, France, and Germany, is not a story of fixity, of merely establishing an Establishment; it is the story of change. It has never, in any year, been quite the same as before. The relationship of people to each other, the relationship of people to their government, the relationship of the different levels of government to each other, the relationship of people to private corporations and the relationship of those corporations to government—in none of these relationships has there been a fixed application of our freedoms.

Nor is there a solid state in other systems of society and government; in those with whom we are allied, or in those with whom we have been at odds. Not only have the "isms" changed since I was a college student, they have been revised drastically in the last ten years. President Nixon's decision to go to Peking was evidence that we no longer have the same view of communism as we did when he was Vice-President. His trip, someone remarked to me, would have been impossible in the days of Senator William Knowland. It would have been unthinkable, I said, in the days of Senator Nixon. This is not just because of change in us. The Communist countries seem to have changed the definition of their objectives, and presumably the means to them. This should not surprise us. If at any given point in human affairs, we could arrive at what we considered the ultimate political wisdom, it would be outmoded within a few years.

So, too, yesterday's freedom leads to today's discipline or sacrifice so that tomorrow's freedom can be still more desirable. If, to give an obvious instance, the people of urban America are to have the same access to clean air as the people of rural America, then the freedom of the people of urban America to move about in private motor vehicles is going to have to be sharply restricted. Rural Americans will have to suffer the same restrictions when they come into the city. You cannot have the same freedom to use the automobile and the highway as you had twenty-five years ago if you are to protect that still more fundamental freedom, the right to draw breath.

The people of rural America are going to have to help pay for urban freedom to breathe, because in doing so, they not only accept their responsibilities as citizens, they protect their own ultimate freedom to breathe. And they preserve the principle that in a democracy we help each other, in the tithing of wealth, in the institutionalized generosity, called taxation.

That is the story of our national existence; the willingness of some people to give up privileges and rewards for others, or, at the least to share them.

As society changes, attitudes change. Agreement on what is in our own best interest changes. So do views of what is right or wrong. My children often appear not to be vastly interested in what we thought of as Fundamental Values when I was their age. One of us is wrong—they or I. I don't have to live indefinitely with my mistakes, while they have much longer to live with theirs. They are not going to live according to what they conceive to be my mistakes, my ancient values; they *are* going to live with their own.

The young are not uninterested in tradition or in history, but they express their interest in different ways. Some young people, I must say, haven't bothered to learn the history they enjoy rejecting. Fair enough, I suppose. I don't enjoy the music of their generation, for the most part, but sometimes when I listen to "my" music, to "our" music, I think I can understand why they don't enjoy it. Maybe that is a step toward enjoying their music. I still have a long way to go.

They have a difference of opinion and of perspective on a

lot of things. I don't know whether this means that they will really use their freedom to pursue their own, improved set of values. I do think it is good to have such impulses in a day when the crowded character of our society tends to inhibit individual freedom. It is good to have strong individuals to counter our culture.

The question I raise, along with many other adults, is whether their response will come to grips with the problems of bringing this splendid, staggering society into a more beneficent order.

One cannot fault young people for going around shouting "Love!" at each other and at us, but that injunction doesn't translate rapidly into legislation, or programs, or money, or action, or even add to the human will to do good. There is a nice motive behind it and a healthy impulse; it remains to be seen whether the young will find ways to carry such sentiments beyond impulse.

Impulse is not enough to overcome problems that stretch beyond today or that affect our lives in different but related ways. That is why I stress that one issue, one theme, one problem cannot be seen alone. If we talk of environment, soon we must talk of poverty. We can't speak of poverty without mentioning the racial malaise involved, or talk of race without education or health. We can talk of none of these without laws, taxes, ideas, money, leadership.

What, for instance, causes poverty? It is not simply that some babies are born poor. They are born to, and live, with other people. God may not have given a particular human being, child or parent, what it takes to succeed in our kind of society—child or parent may carry with him an inheritance of limitations.

And what of people who are born equal to the challenge of their environment and are not given a chance? What creates *those* circumstances? And how do we assure the first child as good a chance at life as the second?

We know that the first child can be born into circumstances where he is not free to develop. But the parallel tragedy is that even if he is born free, in the sense of having a healthy brain and body, and with loving parents, we have not yet devised all the possible ways for him to grow fully.

As we devise those ways, we must be prepared to cope with the changes they will bring, for we will be changing the situation of those on the lower rungs of opportunity's ladder, who either don't know how to look up, or who, looking up, can only see a lot of ladder. People clinging weakly to bottom rungs are not much given to philosophical debate on such questions. When they look—and reach—up they want to climb. If they can't, there's trouble. But a deeper, graver problem is that we have those who do not know enough to look or to reach. Some people fear change; some agitate for it; I worry about those who do not know (or believe) yet that substantial change is possible.

We see, then, another form of poverty: the absence of dreams, of ambitions. Again, I feel most deeply for those who do not know what they are missing.

There are Americans living lives that give them little reason to harbor hope. The first thing they do not own is the ability to conceive of something better. And that is the deadly part of such a life. I am as concerned about the poverty of hope as I am about the distance to the dream's realization. Conservatives, who might take comfort in the fact that only a minority of any minority is militant, fool themselves. If you deprive people of even the means to dream, particularly in a social order where the contrasts between their condition and someone else's can be so grave and so visible, they are not going to accept what they've got, even without realizable objectives. Expectations are dangerous when aroused without a chance of satisfaction. The truism fits; it is easier to keep a man a slave than it is to keep him half free. But a dearth of expectations can be dangerous, too.

If a man has a sense of his own identity, heritage, and capacity, he will take risks to realize them. The chance must be there to open up whatever creative energies he may have, the energies that can give life meaning. A person may not know what these stirrings are inside him, but the fact that something stirs could be the first impulse and impetus to take off. I believe that the educators are right, that if the promptings and possibilities of awakening intelligence are most fragile and most vital in the first five years, then we must make certain that these stirrings survive the first years.

The contrasts I have noted are part of a tragic landscape as some of us journey on while others stay in place. In Manhattan, the levels of life to be seen harshly contrasted within a few short blocks, along the Upper East Side and through the Upper West Side, are sobering. In Hong Kong, I was struck by the desperate disparity between the fine homes on the hillside and the misery of those on the water. You could jump from one to the other. But most people cannot make that jump. In Rio, the poor have the heights of the hill, with the best and worst view of the wealth below. Such lines of contrast are the lines of tension. It is sad that we may have the means to meet the problem, but we haven't yet found the methods or even the will.

Another sadness is the question of deferred high hopes, of expectations. In recent years we have heard of one bit of advice suggesting that demands for equal opportunity be met with benign neglect. This is an idea that the British once had in response to their troubles in the colonies and Canada. One of the czars allowed a breath of freedom to tantalize the nostrils of the oppressed, with revolutionary results. Yet the twin truths are that we must be concerned with making certain that people have the right to hope as well as the right to know how much they can expect to achieve in their lifetime. Do we dare to let them sleep and wake only in nightmare bursts? I am convinced that despite the dangers of overpromising, we can match the dream with the reality of the awakening.

Encouraging a dream is not the same as presenting unrealizable ambition or expectation.

One cruel expectation, I think, is the promised Vietnam dividend—the "war dividend." Perhaps many people are realistic about it and know that much of that dividend will probably never exist. Yet I grieve for those who think, because they have been told, that once the war is over for us, once we have extricated ourselves, the funds can be applied like a poultice to our domestic problems, "solving" poverty, race, education, taxation, inflation.

Whatever war dividend there might be has largely disappeared because of inflation and because of commitments to new weapons systems. But even without that factor, the "saving" probably was never as real as some of us were told. The promised future fiscal-social dividend in ending the war has also been an excuse for some. It was a way of avoiding the sacrifice and expense of doing our duty here at home, now.

We cannot eliminate all the costs of security, war or no war, and much of the balance could be illusory. Whatever real savings there might be after we disengage from war, any experienced leader knows that it is not easy to make the necessary political processes work for social ends. The legislators who support war expenditures and who are strongest for a strong military posture are seldom the same as those who support appropriations for better housing.

There is also the problem of the populace. After exerting the effort and paying the price in sons and dollars to prosecute an unpopular cause and to form alliances with an ally who never commanded our allegiance, people want to be relieved of the burden, not to have it shifted. So there will be the popular as well as the political reaction to contend with. To imply that expenditures are easily transferable from munitions to munificence is neither realistic nor compassionate.

President Johnson and his advisers announced a "war on poverty." But almost no one approaches poverty as if it were an active enemy of the people, which it is, and we do not attack it as we would visible aggression by an alien force. Calling for a war on poverty produces few volunteers and it is difficult, as always, to draft the unwilling.

Unfortunately, we didn't know enough in Lyndon Johnson's time about how you "fight" poverty. I'm not sure we do now. The call to battle was timely, given the need, but it may have been early, given the results. Still, it was a call to experimentation and should have been recognized as such, rather than a call to follow a well-developed battle plan, because nobody had one. And such plans as were created soon were caught in the Vietnam War. Whether or not we could have funded our future as well as the war is another question. In any case, the experiments might have worked out better if the funds had not begun to shrink.

This is true of many domestic programs that Lyndon Johnson initiated, and he ought to be given great credit for them. The only way a free society can work is to experiment with the uses of its freedom. If you hear a manifesto by someone who professes to have all the answers, you can be certain that the answers, and likely the leader, are phony.

The distinguishing quality of a great free society is its freedom to experiment, freedom to make mistakes, freedom to change direction, freedom to back away from failure and to enlarge on success.

This is what President Johnson was willing to risk in the case of his domestic ideas and, eventually, in the great gray issue of the war. Certain programs that he recommended and pushed through the Congress were not successes. But he clearly *identified* the areas where our nation needed to make the most effort—such issues as racial tensions, voting rights, urban problems, poverty, hunger, violence, race, schools, and environmental matters. Going down through that list one can see that it was an unprecedented set of urgent priorities that he identified, labeled, and began to put through. Where he and the programs of the Great Society were pulled down was through our deepening, distracting, enervating involvement in Vietnam, a war that I and a majority of Americans now regard as a mistake. This war limited Lyndon Johnson's freedom to follow through on his domestic initiatives. But those initiatives were aimed at the heart of our problems and came from the heart. He did not have the answers to every problem. But he was willing to try. The war was his tragedy and thus, in that period, ours.

When we consider our great expectations, we must consider not only the expectations and the understandings of those we would help but of those who have to provide the help. I don't mean the professionals; I mean the ordinary citizen, which in our country means the extraordinary person who pays the bills—and sometimes the piper.

Frequently, every public man hears the private comment that welfare means Cadillacs parked outside of shabby houses, with absentee or non-existent fathers. The stock answers are no help. Groups of ethnic Americans, such as my own, are apt to be resentful of a situation if the truth has been distorted. "Well, *we* made it because we were willing to work. We had to work against discrimination, injustice, and so on, but we were willing to work and we worked hard. And we've made a place for ourselves." That place is now threatened by others, they think, and it doesn't seem fair. "We give them a chance to work; they're entitled to that—but what you fellows are doing is giving handouts."

Blacks, among others, resent this because their instant reaction is that "There's nothing in your experience which is like ours." Resentment flares and smolders on both sides, which makes truth, like progress, hard to detect. There can be no explaining away the Cadillacs or the lazy, wherever they may exist. But I don't think that we can create virtue by forcing people to go hungry, or snap off programs because abusers exist. A government "handout" is a painful paycheck. The welfare rolls do not include a high proportion of people who refuse to work. I believe that most of the people on welfare would rather work than stay on it—and there is evidence to back up this opinion. But beyond data, I have found that people who live in circumstances where there is little hope of betterment, circumstances where whatever work is available produces little income or other job satisfactions, find the public paycheck a grim experience. If those who work their hearts out get little more than bare subsistence and zero psychic income, then over a period of time some will say, "Why work?" If sweeping up trash or raking leaves at seventy-six dollars a week is the alternative to a government check of seventy-five dollars, the temptation to take the second check is understandable. When welfare income and the only prospects of earned income are roughly the same, one begins to wonder indeed, why work? Many of us have worked for too little at times, but we had the feeling we were

on the way up. Those who are condemned to live at the base
of the ladder, to subsist rather than live, are going to be
tempted to avoid a climb on which they likely will be lost.
The responsibility, then, is not just theirs. The responsibility
is ours to create an environment in which they can improve
themselves—and believe it.

Little hope to advance, underdeveloped skills or no skills,
a lack of education, transportation, and incentive: This
profile of life in America, which is the portion of some of our
citizens, is hardly the silhouette of The American Way. It
does not stimulate new Horatio Alger stories in the imagination. This is the dead end on a journey to nowhere.

Our failure in the cities is particularly acute because cities
have been the real centers of life, and more than a few are
sick, if not dying. Where people mass together, the depressing evidence reinforces the desperation, antagonism—or
apathy.

I believe that most people, if helped at the right age to see
a chance to journey ahead, are willing to start almost anywhere. They are willing to work a treadmill as long as it is
not the infamous one to oblivion. I believe this to be true of
Black Americans as well as white Americans. I believe it
to be true of any ethnic or racial group. I believe it to be true
of any society faintly resembling our own.

CHAPTER VI

●

Toward Equality

BECAUSE I care, and care to the core of my being, about those who have been denied an equal chance in our society, I should explain how I came to my present view and feelings. It would be dramatic to say, I suppose, that I had a history of personal persecution that gave me an instant feeling of brotherhood with Blacks, Indians, Spanish-speaking Americans, Mexican-Americans, and others. Only truth stands in the way. To a certain extent my identification with their problems is geared to my own, but not in the way one might suppose.

There were no Blacks in the town in which I grew up. My family was part of one minority group in the town, but there was no rough persecution and little overt evidence of our "inferiority."

We lived in an area where there were Poles, Lithu-
anians, some French, Irish, and Yankees. The Italians lived
in another part of town. All the "ethnics" were looked
down on for a while in a period after World War I, and I had
the feeling that those of us from Eastern and Northern
Europe were more subject to discrimination than the French.
I can remember when the Ku Klux Klan was alive and active
in Maine in the 1920s, and I can remember the derision with
which the term "Pollock" was used.

There had been a strong tradition of anti-slavery in
Maine. Our state had been in the forefront of the abolitionist
movement. Elijah Parish Lovejoy, a martyr in the abolition
movement, was from Maine. Harriet Beecher Stowe wrote
Uncle Tom's Cabin in Brunswick, Maine, and General
Oliver Howard, head of the Freedman's Bureau after the
Civil War and founder of Howard University, was a Maine
native. Maine lost many of its sons in the Civil War and it
was one of the strong founding states for the original Republican Party. All of the traditions for believing in equal rights
were there, but mostly at a distance. By and large, mine was
for a long time an intellectual commitment. I had been
raised in a family culture of equality, fairness, justice, opportunity, and those values seemed to me values that all men
were entitled to share. My convictions did not come from
any great exposure to the pain of prejudice.

My first view of Black ghetto life in America came when,
as a child, I visited my aunt and uncle in South Boston, on
West Brookline Street, close to Roxbury, where much of the
Black population lived. I was too young to get a clear picture
of the relationships between the groups there, but I had
some sense of the tensions that existed.

I remained largely ignorant of real racial discrimination
through my high school years. The first step in my awareness

and the start of any emotional commitment was in college. Bates had a policy at that time of what might be called "controlled open admissions." It was a quota system. The college allowed in two Blacks every year, out of a student body of seven hundred. The Blacks who made it were, of course, men of outstanding quality, the selection process was so exacting. Dr. Benjamin May was one of Bates's distinguished Black students. The Blacks were highly visible, well liked, and very much part of the college community. I discovered the first evidence of prejudice in my experience when we named one of the two men as class marshal for the Junior Class exercises. An anonymous letter arrived protesting his appointment and threatening to make an issue of it. We had a meeting of our small committee and decided to stick to our guns. It was a small matter, in today's context, but it wasn't inconsequential then, and certainly not to Jim Carter, the man involved. Jim afterward went into politics. He is a member of the Illinois legislature and is Commissioner of Public Vehicle Licenses in the city of Chicago.

Our other classmate, Owen Dodson, became a poet and playwright. He taught for a time at Howard University and is now at the Harlem School of the Arts, New York City.

My experience at college was highly selective and hardly a firsthand acquaintance with what it was to be Black in America. I met and became friends with two good men who were Black. My experience with them and my encounter with that incident in college only confirmed what was instinctive. I didn't know there was anything special about believing that men and women ought to be able to live as equals.

During World War II, my first assignment on board a ship was as a supply officer on a destroyer escort. I had some training and experience in the engineering department, so I asked the captain if I could get back into engineering, rather than supply. He took me off supply.

While the ship was in the Navy Yard for repairs, we had the usual disciplinary problems. One involved a steward's mate, who was Black. The complaining officer was, as it happened, from Maine. The steward's mate had been charged with disobeying an order and was to be given a court-martial, and I was assigned to him as counsel. I was more than willing, but the prosecutor was more than able. There was a board of three officers and they found the mate guilty. I got the distinct feeling that the decision was controlled more by the sense that an officer was the complaining officer than by a balanced view of the rights of the enlisted man. That the incident also involved a Black man troubled me. Such feelings ought to not rule the law, I felt, and I did not think the mate was guilty. I suffered from my own bias, of course, which was that of the lawyer defending a client and of a man who believed in another man. In that case, I had a glimpse at racial prejudice, but it was only a glimpse.

I didn't run into race as an issue until I entered the Senate. The first civil rights legislation in a century was enacted in Congress in 1957, and then later, in 1959, when I was new in the Senate, we had the change of Rule 22, which is related to the whole question of civil rights legislation.* And so I found myself on the line, voting against the Majority Leader for an amendment to Rule 22 that would make it easier to end filibusters. Consistently, from that time on, I have supported civil rights legislation.

In the Senate, as a member of the Banking and Currency

---

* Rule 22 of the Senate governs limitations on debate. For years it was successfully used by anti-civil rights senators to forestall efforts to end filibusters.

Committee, I soon encountered the issue of fair housing; that is, of integrated housing or fair access to decent living quarters. The question of subsidized housing to meet social needs was much tougher ten years ago than it is today. This kind of housing involved high budgetary costs, rather than questions of subsidies for housing that would be financed largely in the private market.

Public housing is not an exact synonym for ethnic or racial housing, but it is related. Before I came to the Senate it was understood that the best way to get at so-called social housing, housing relating to social needs, was to tie it in omnibus housing legislation, to Federal Housing Administration authorizations and amendments. FHA was a way of subsidizing housing for the middle class and the affluent. It didn't work very well to meet the needs of the poor and the deprived, so we always managed in every omnibus housing bill to put a price on that legislation, the price being social housing. And the possibilities for doing so increased as the years went by. Not until the 1968 Act did we get what I would call a really good piece of legislation and there is still a long way to go. For the first time we embraced the concept of home ownership for the poor, which would have been unthinkable in the years just before. We still haven't dealt effectively with the problem by any means, but we have at least secured solid acceptance of the notion that the government should do what it can to open up housing ownership to the poor as well as to the middle class. Sometimes a small step takes us a long way.

From my first years as senator, I believed that for minorities, as for majorities, the ballot is of first importance. It was the basic objective to achieve in those days. Voting rights were fundamental first, and those who pressed for them, with commitment and dedication, were right to do so. We fell short as a nation by not pressing forward at the same time as effectively as we could have on other fronts. In any case, it was important to get voting rights legislation through and some of the political results justify that judgment. The fact that Blacks in the southern states are being registered now, the fact that they are running for office, the fact that they are being elected to office, is having, a very visible and important effect upon public opinion. There are moments of disillusion or disappointment with the setbacks in some big cities, such as those affecting the mayors of Newark, Gary, and East St. Louis. They start with the standard problems of all mayors, and they are blamed for not achieving for their constituents what had been hoped. In addition, they have achieved political power at a time when their cities' resources are at their lowest ebb.

It is true, of course, that there is no direct line between voting and getting what you want. And I suppose Blacks have to learn that as well as whites. We are all frustrated by it at times and some Blacks are going to believe that the voting process is meaningless. But it isn't meaningless, even though periods of disillusionment are inevitable. Blacks themselves are increasingly impressed that more and more Blacks are voting and that the fact that they are voting or registering to vote has an impact not only on the fortunes of Black candidates but also upon the attitudes of white political figures. White southern politicians are remarkably different in attitude than those observed a dozen years ago. The changing attitudes of Blacks and whites are important as they exert pressures and develop momentum. The problem is that, Black or white, we don't have all or even many of the answers yet. We haven't developed answers to how you govern cities efficiently and fairly. For example: How do you get at the distortions in housing, job, industrial, educational, and transportation patterns? Every city shows this. You see it in the Polish, German, and Italian ghettos in our northern cities. Those have not been fully integrated yet. But at least the barriers against these ethnic groups are less well enforced than they are with Black people. The barriers which separate will continue to exist, until the mobility which comes with equal opportunity and growing material affluence also has its effect. The opening-up process has only begun but it is very real. Some people think that ghettos are inevitable, citing the natural human tendency to huddle together, but any natural tendency to huddle has long been artificially stimulated by the inhospitability displayed in other parts of the community.

I have minimized the slights of my own life, and with reason. There were, of course, certain things I "understood." At the time I became a candidate I was told that a Catholic could not hope to be elected Governor of Maine, up to that point no Polish-American had been elected governor of any state. I was quite aware of these facts. They were accepted traditions; neither was meant to be personal. And that may be the greatest sin of all, the treatment of a minority group member as a non-person. It was something that came out of the nation's past. The time was ripe and we knocked each barrier down, without ever making much of a point that there was a tradition under attack. In that sense, I've been aware all my life of limitations enforced at one point or another on Poles, Catholics, Democrats, poor people, foreigners. I was aware of these limitations because I was a member of each of these minority groups, but I escaped the period when generalized prejudices were translated into direct personal snubs. Now, I must admit that it has been an asset when people say that "He's the first Polish-American ever elected governor of his state"; or "He's the first Catholic." But I've been sensitive to the fact that these assets could also turn out to be limitations on unity and the healing process. When I went into Massachusetts after being elected governor I was introduced there to Massachusetts Poles in City Hall in Worcester as the first Polish-American ever elected governor of a state. There were lusty cheers. But when I stood up I said that one point should be understood: People didn't vote against me because I was a Polish-American—but neither did they vote for me because I was a Polish-American. And that, to me, was a point that had to be made, because my election signified that perhaps we had reached the point where anybody, regardless of who he was, could be regarded as an American, neither discriminated for nor discriminated against. That was the landmark to me, for a man who had been lucky enough to come of age in the transitional period between personal snub and group insult.

We are a diverse people and you don't eliminate diversity in creating an open society; diversity enriches the society. You don't wipe away differences simply because you fight for equal treatment; you don't want to melt away all differences. That is one of the things Black Americans are talking about. When on the campuses they ask for Black courses, Black faculties, Black history, Black culture studies, they want to establish their identity, their contribution, actual and potential, to this culture, and to see and show their roots and heritage. It's important that Black Americans, Spanish-speaking, Indian, and other Americans accomplish these aims, that they have opportunities to do so, even if some pioneering efforts misfire.

I do not want to appear to stretch my sense of personal identity with the problems of Blacks too far. Discrimination is not the same for Blacks as it is or was for people of other ethnic or national or religious groupings. To be Black means that you cannot "pass" just by curing your accent and working hard. To be here because one's forebears came as slaves is radically different from being here because your ancestors came here to be free. Although other foreigners were treated as inferiors, I suspect that the assumption was not as entrenched that there was basic biological or physiological inferiority. The Blacks especially have suffered from such assumptions.

The notion of biological "inferiority" dies hard, but it is dying. You cannot quantify this feeling, but I doubt very much that such notions are as widely or as deeply held as they once were. One still runs into it. And it's widespread enough to be a dead trunk lying across the tortuous path to racial equality in this country. It is still widely enough held to be the basis for the fears that restrain people from reaching out to Blacks and helping to pull down the barriers. Too often barriers are seen as barricades, or as protection; not just economic protection but protection against "inferior" standards of education for one's own children; "inferior" standards of conduct; "inferior" values. That is why the education of whites is important along with increased educational opportunities for Blacks. People who still base their bigotry on belief in biological inferiority are themselves suffering from a handicap, which is underdeveloped sensitivity. That may forgive some of them too easily, because people with an opportunity to be educated, as well as some college-educated people believe this. It has to be a primordial instinct on their part.

The fear of busing is also a protective instinct, one that Blacks *and* whites each experience with respect to their young. Most Blacks don't like the idea of busing any better than most whites. There is not only the protective instinct; there is also the question of just how much of a child's time each day ought to be consumed in transportation to and from school, and of what the child finds at the other end of the line after school, as well as in it. The next question promotes fears too. Hours of commuting time, followed by what? Friendship and companionship, or social separation enforced by busing.

There ought to be a better answer. And yet with the fixed housing and transportation and political boundaries and barriers that are established no easy answer has been found.

What is really desirable here is mobility, the means to make a change. Not all Blacks would take advantage of mobility. But they want to feel that the possibility is there —that they are free to move different ways. Free to send their children to better schools or free to live in a different neighborhood. We have to find ways of making mobility real and of persuading Americans, of whatever color, that it is. The reason that mobility has become an important element in educating children is because *de jure* segregation in the South physically separated the two races in the schools and *de facto* segregation in the North caused the same result. And so in order to integrate you have to have mobile children—unless you move the schools. There is no single or simple answer in southern or northern cities. New school districts, new schools and relocated boundaries, better facilities, and better teachers are all needed. They cannot be provided without more money, but in the absence of that kind of investment, the courts have turned to busing to move children from one side of the city to the other, from the central city to the suburbs and back again. As of this writing, the Supreme Court has not ordered busing to achieve racial balance, indicating its awareness of the limitations of busing as a means of achieving full mobility. Those limitations are real.

Busing is not, in the first instance, a problem of education. It is the penalty for segregated housing. Thus, you just can't avoid the distances if you want to achieve integration. And you can't handily move the houses or the schools, though you can change the lines of school districts. But when you are talking about a city the size of Washington—Black inside and white outside—how do you achieve an equitable mix? We do not yet have the final answers, but we cannot and should not attempt to go back to the old days of "separate but equal." And I am convinced that the answer requires full mobility for all Americans.

The conventional rhetoric about discrimination always speaks in terms of minorities, or at least it used to. I find a phrase appearing more and more in my talks against inequality: the minority who are Black and brown and the majority who are women. It can be a cliché, but it is an important reminder, for me and for my audience. And we do need to remind ourselves over and over again of the ways in which women suffer from thoughtless customs as well as the outmoded laws of our society. I do not expect to get a 100 per cent rating from the advocates of Ms., because I must deal with the habits of a lifetime (as they must); but I am learning, and largely from a wife who had always been a help in my campaigns but who in this election year has achieved her own independence as a campaigner.

I have no difficulty in urging an end to discriminating laws against women and in supporting the Equal Rights Amendment to the Constitution. It is quite easy for me to make the public commitment to appoint women to high places in the executive and judicial branches of government, if I am elected. I can, without reservation, press for equal opportunity for women in education and in the professions.

But I would be less than candid if I did not admit that implementing each of these steps requires a conscious effort. That is the last, toughest barrier to equality, for women and for minorities. Intellectual judgment about the wrongs of inequality and injustice is not so hard to achieve, but the emotional commitments require some discomfort if we are to overcome life-long, ages-old patterns that have become far too comfortable for those of us who have been privileged.

Despite my good luck, it is no wonder that my upbringing, my natural inclinations, and my political experiences have caused me to side with the other minorities and the female majority. I do understand, although I do not enjoy the fact, that frustrations, ignorance, innocence, and pent-up rage often result in explosions of violence. The demonstrable historical truth, much as we would love to avoid it, is that violence sometimes has achieved action, first, attention and then positive results, that nothing else had been able to produce. Yet, violence as a rule or routine answer to solving social problems is madness. Violence ultimately or suddenly turns back against the violent. When I hear calls to violence as the answer to all our national problems I recoil, because like other Americans, I have seen too much of sudden death in our time.

In 1968, we saw two young men, committed to change and committed to peace, cut down by violent acts.

I never knew Martin Luther King but I had much admiration from the start for what he was attempting in his insistence on non-violence as he struggled to improve the quality of life for the Blacks of our country. Later, and especially, I admired his steadfastness in the face of growing militancy, the pressure from some of his own followers, and the absolute and unyielding opposition of some of his foes. I admired the courage he carried with him in support of his ideals. For those whose frustration seeks not only expression but action to deal with injustice, Martin Luther King, Jr., building on the non-violent tradition of Gandhi, revealed a viable alternative to violence.

On hearing of Dr. King's assassination, I decided to go to Atlanta for the funeral. I learned that there was a small congressional delegation assembly and so I set off with Senators Philip Hart and Frank Moss and others. It was an explosive, tense atmosphere in those somber hours. Leaving Washington, we didn't know what we might encounter in Georgia, whether we would run into active hostility, rejection, or indifference. What we ran into was a solemn, moving experience.

Met at the plane by buses, we piled into them and headed for the Ebenezer Baptist Church. Huge crowds were everywhere but we had little difficulty reaching the area. As we approached, we were engulfed by a sea of people. We got closer to the church, but soon learned that there was no possibility of getting into it. We waited then, there in the sun, and watched Mrs. King arrive and enter, and soon we could hear the services begin.

Among the things we heard was the sermon he had preached in that church, not long before the assassination, when he said, in part:

"Every now and then, I guess we all think realistically about that day when we will be victimized with what is life's final common denominator—that something we call death. We all think about it and every now and then I think about my own death and . . . my own funeral. And I don't think in a morbid sense . . . "I don't want a long funeral. And if you get somebody

to deliver the eulogy, tell him not to talk too long. . . .
"I'd like somebody to mention that day that Martin
Luther King, Jr., tried to give his life serving others.
I'd like for somebody to say that Martin Luther King,
Jr., tried to love somebody. . . ."

He wouldn't have any money to leave behind, said Dr. King.
But, he added, "I just want to leave a committed life behind."

He had done that. And more.

Toward the end of the service, a few of us did manage to
squeeze into a balcony, where we could see the pulpit and
the casket at the front of the church. After the service,
a farm wagon and donkeys were brought up to the church,
and the crowd was cleared back a bit so that the casket
could be brought out and placed on the wagon. We were
now put in the front rank of those who were to march.
At least it was the front rank for a time. Gradually, we
were pushed back somewhat. But the senators and congressmen who were with us formed a complete line from one
curb to another. We were led by a Black clergyman with
a monumental singing voice and a great presence, and as
we walked we became a part of his family on that long
march.

I forget how long it was. At times it seemed like miles
and the sun was hot, but we sang all the songs. "We
Shall Overcome" was the favorite. And nowhere was there
any hostility. We were at home from the beginning, our
fellow Black citizens accepting us in this, our shared moment
of sorrow. Water along the line of march became a problem.
That was solved when people ran inside their houses and
brought it out. Somewhere in the course of that journey
we reached a height and could look back a long straight

road. It was unbelievable, the masses of people, Black people as far back as you could see and as far ahead. I found the march to be tiring but not exhausting, a cleansing, uplifting of the spirit.

In the wake of the funeral and the riots that followed Martin Luther King's death, I hoped that the anguish of his loss would dampen the fire of violence that had cost us a President and a spiritual leader within five short years. That hope died too soon, also.

When Robert Kennedy was killed in Los Angeles, I experienced deep feelings of personal regret. Perhaps my response was akin to that of many other Americans: Sorrow not only at the loss of so young and so promising a man, and the savage hurt to a wounded family, but a sadness that I hadn't gotten to know him better. I had known President Kennedy as a friend. I had not been close to Robert, and had really just begun to know him when we were all caught up in the campaign—and then he was gone. My loss was keen and personal, all the more so, curiously, because we had not been close.

As I got to know more about him, Bobby Kennedy seemed to me a tremendous human being, with a great heart, concerned, and, like King, courageous. Most of all, he was a passionate and compassionate man who understood that orderly and timely change doesn't just happen. He tried, particularly in those last few months before his death, to channel the driving forces for change into a constructive political movement. He understood that the alternative to orderly change is violence which, if it persists, hardens and toughens the lines between people and encourages repression.

The answer is that orderly process must be made *truly* responsive. Due process must not translate as glacial progress.

Despite constant talk of change and revolution, the affairs of man move sickeningly slowly at times. Improvements were started in the thirties that are still not finished. The welfare reform program is one such. We went from the county poorhouse or "farm" of those days in the early thirties to the Social Security Act, Unemployment Compensation, and related measures of great consequence. Yet these designs were for *transitional* programs to help us work toward new institutions to create a more humane order. Social Security benefits never reached the level where people could live on them, and constant inflation, aggravated by three wars, meant that the "supplementary Old-Age Assistance Program," devised as a temporary measure of the thirties, endures today in the seventies. We haven't yet finished the reform that we started, although we can all thank God that political pressure makes the endeavor endure and be at least minimally responsive to the needs of old people. The benefits have never been plush. They have always lagged behind what older Americans need to live on. And we must complete the job of making retirement years the years of dignity and security.

Changes are often begun but are seldom finished. We experience just enough calculated change to take the pressure off changing; then everyone rests on his oars for a while and matters go half reformed. One could make the case, I suppose, that not all reform *should* be completed. Half measures are adequate in certain cases. But we must take maximum advantage of the impulse to change when it exists and we should do as workmanlike and complete a job as we can at that point.

Presidents are elected often in response to some inclination for change, even if it's for a change back to "normalcy." But a President has just so much time to put his stamp on the country, perhaps three or four years. For all practical purposes, Franklin Roosevelt had four years. The major domestic institutions created by the New Deal had been dealt out by 1936. In President Kennedy's case, his appeal was, at least in part, to those who responded to the idea of getting the country moving forward again. With President Eisenhower, the country, by and large, wanted a minimum of federal action, almost inaction, it sometimes seems, to follow the years of intense action and reaction that preceded him. This seemed to coincide with his own views of the presidency. If the pace was pretty slow, if he didn't inundate the Congress with proposals, that is presumably because he thought the country wanted it that way. He had the political power to achieve more change than any President in my lifetime, with the possible exception of Franklin Roosevelt, and very likely General Eisenhower had greater power over a longer period. But to use that power, at least overtly, was not his instinct. Perhaps that is why, in the long run, he had and retained power. In other words, for Presidents, at least, power unused is greater than power used: It is a limited capital reserve that must be spent wisely. My own conviction is that it must be spent without hesitation to deal with injustice and inequality.

Late in 1971, I uttered an opinion in private which some thought was a mistake. When talking with a group of Black leaders in Los Angeles, I was asked about a Black running mate and I said that I did not believe that if I became my party's presidential nominee that we could win with such a slate. This was quickly carried on the wires and warped in transmission. The propaganda had it that I didn't want a Black running mate, wouldn't accept one, and didn't think a Black should seek high office.

I regret the misunderstandings of my response, but what I was trying to say was important to get across. It still is. The point, simply, is that there is prejudice in this country which denies to Blacks their fullest political opportunities. We need to focus on this fact, on a pattern of discrimination which is eroding but which is still entrenched in our national life. Unless we are willing to face facts, we can't come to grips with problems—and eliminate their causes. I deplore the situation of which I spoke. The statement I made was an opinion, not a decision.

There are so many objectives which we seek to achieve: the kind of upward turn in health care, for example, which will alter the hard stark facts that Black infants have a 40 per cent chance of dying before they reach their forty-fifth birthday; that unemployment is twice as high among Blacks as among whites; that our Black children do not have nearly the same chance as our white children for an education of fairly high quality. Surely, these conditions need to be changed. The question is: How do we move effectively to correct these facts and in what order do we take them up? If having a Black on the national presidential ticket is more important, then we can give such a move high priority. I want every American to be as eligible for office as I am—or, more precisely, as I became. The day I was born, someone of my background could not be seen as a serious, electable candidate for the presidency. The change is a gain for me but it is a greater gain for the nation. I want such a change for our Black citizens as well.

There are Black men and women now, some of them in elective office, who have the qualifications. I don't want them to have to wait another lifetime for a chance at still a higher office. But the President responded to the news of my remark by saying: "I believe it is frankly a libel on the American people." He went on to say, it was reported, that it was important not to tell a large number of people in America that they don't have a chance to go to the top. I thought it was a tribute to the people with whom I was talking (and, as it turned out, to Americans generally) to rely once more on their ability to deal with problems by looking at them squarely. Mark Twain once said, "Truth is a precious thing. Use it sparingly." I think of this remark sometimes but I don't think truth should be used as sparingly as it has been in national politics of late.

There is, I think, a hunger in our land for belief, belief in leadership, belief in institutions, and I'll go on trying to seek and speak the truth whenever I can discover it and spell it out. I am going to fall short of this ideal but I will continue to try. I do not want to pretend that because one's objective is truth and honesty that one is necessarily possessed of all truth.

There are politicians who oversimplify racial issues, and who think that with a backward-looking southern strategy they can gain the South. Such an attitude insults and divides the South and the nation. The conventional assumption is that a Democrat who cares about human and civil rights can never carry the South. That assumption is wrong. The time has long gone when a candidate could justify going into the South and be afraid to say what he knows is right.

Color does not divide humanity. People divide humanity. Deprivation and despair are color blind. No southern strategy can divide the Black worker from the white worker if each share the common emptiness of unemployment, if each is a partner in failure.

If I am nominated for the highest office in the land, and if it should be God's will that I am given such responsibility, then it would have to be with the clear understanding that I am going to reach out to every American and make him feel welcome in this land. I don't intend to become, or to be used, as a barrier or a shield against other Americans. And I am going to do so, because it serves each of us, all of us, including the unborn, to carry our country farther along the rocky road to equality.

Trouble? Difficult adjustments? Our Gross National Product? As it happens, I believe that a better United States will also create a better GNP. History couldn't care less, a thousand years from now, if we have a trillion dollar GNP in 1972. But if our achievement is a stride, not a step, toward equality in our time, then we are all rich beyond dreams. And history will know why we were here.

CHAPTER VII

●

Political Responsibilities

MY FIRST VENTURE in politics came shortly after the war.
I had returned to Waterville ready to pick up my law practice
where I had left off. I was not overwhelmed with clients and
it was obvious that there was plenty of work to do if I was
going to build up a healthy practice in my one-man
office. (Those clients I still had following the war were mine
largely through the attention and good sense of my secretary, Mrs. Marjorie Hutchinson.) I took some interest in
civic and local political activities, as most young lawyers do,
but I had no burning desire to become an active leader or
candidate for public office. But I was young, presentable, and
a veteran, and the Democrats of Waterville were looking
for legislative candidates who fitted that description. In the
spring of 1946, I was called on by a good friend, Harold

Dubord, who had been a distinguished leader in the Maine Democratic Party. He asked me to run for a seat that was held by a Republican.

I ran, and I was elected. No one was more surprised than I.

There were very few Democrats in that ninety-third legislature: twenty-four out of 151 in the House of Representatives and three out of thirty-three in the Senate. In the next legislature, elected in 1948, we reached twenty-five members in the House and five in the Senate, and in that legislature I was elected House Minority Leader. It was a post without much power. The majority made all the committee assignments and they were careful to keep the Democrats off most of the important committees. We had no staff and no fixed meeting place we could call our own. It was a rigorous training ground for minority politics.

In 1950, I was faced with a decision about my personal and political future. My family and my law practice were growing, and I felt an obligation to tend to both. At the same time, I felt a responsibility to my constituency and the Democratic Party. Finally I went to see an older Republican friend and counselor, Harvey Eaton. He heard me out, looked me in the eye and said: "If you are going to be in this world, Muskie, you might as well be part of it." I decided to run, and I was re-elected to the legislature by *one* vote in a Republican landslide year. I was again elected House Minority Leader by my twenty-three colleagues (we dropped to two members in the Senate that year), but in 1951 I was invited to head the Office of Price Stabilization for Maine. It wasn't the most popular office available at the time, but I remembered my friend's advice. That assignment took me all over the state of Maine, investigating consumer complaints, checking pricing practices, and reasoning with farmers and businessmen who were upset with the price control bureaucracy. We were in the middle of the Korean war, then, and patriotic appeals had some effect, but it was not easy to make the system work fairly or efficiently. (I take some comfort from the fact that within three years of being director of the price control program in the state of Maine, I could be elected governor.)

My two guiding principles as OPS director were fairness and reason. If government is neither fair nor reasonable, no amount of power or enforcement personnel will make the system work effectively for very long. If customers, wholesalers (including farmers), or retailers believe that the price-control mechanism is rigged against them, they will give only token co-operation. Regulatory or personnel gaps will be exploited by some, creating further confusion and resentment. Controls are never desirable, however necessary they may be, but where they are applied the government has an obligation to do all it can to insure against inequitable treatment. This depends on attitude and the adequacy of the machinery set up to operate the program. I am afraid that the Nixon administration, which resisted the idea of restraints on wage and price decisions for so long, was not really prepared to do all it could or would to implement an adequate and fair price-wage control program.

In 1952, I returned to private practice and politics, being elected Democratic national committeeman for Maine and taking an active part in Adlai Stevenson's campaign for President. Our resources were limited in Maine, but we did what we could to help in a gallant race. At a time when the fortunes and prospects of the Democratic Party were bleak, Adlai Stevenson inspired us with his idealism, his eloquence, and his commitment to "talk sense" to the American people. We are still benefiting from his example, and I am still warmed by the memory of the friendship I came to have with him.

The following year while remodeling our home in Waterville, I nearly ended my career and my life. When Jane and I married in 1948, we bought a modest, one-and-a-half-story Cape Cod house. It was ideal for a young couple, but four years and two children later we needed more room. I finished two rooms on the second floor and completed the stairs. One day I leaned back against the stair railing to admire my handiwork. The railing gave way and I ended up in the hospital with a broken back. Since then I have been reluctant to step back to appraise my work, literally or figuratively.

Exercise and a back brace enabled me to get back to work and to resume my law practice and my politicking, just about in time to get swept up in the 1954 campaign. That year, a few of us decided that the Maine Democratic Party did not need to remain a permanent minority. At the March convention, Frank M. Coffin, a young lawyer, had changed the party's method of writing a platform from a back-room, small-committee affair to a voter-participation project. He was elected to the State Committee and became the state chairman. He was determined to build a team of candidates in that election, and although I had doubts about my own physical capacity for campaigning so soon after a back injury, I shared his conviction and determination. We had an announced candidate for the First District congressional seat, but we needed candidates for governor, senator, and the two other congressional seats. My first instinct was to run for Congress, but after a number of fruitless calls to other prospects, I agreed to take on the incumbent governor. The search for candidates had all the attributes of *The Perils of Pauline,* and we barely made the filing deadlines for the

primary. Our team included a former Republican congressman, James C. Oliver (First District), a young lawyer,
Thomas E. Delahanty (Second District), a businessman,
Kenneth B. Colbath (Third District), a college history professor, Paul A. Fullam (Senate), and me. The odds against
us were very great. Maine had not elected a Democratic
governor or congressman in twenty years, and we had never
had a popularly elected senator in the history of the state.
Our funds matched our prospects. In June, when Frank
Coffin started up a full-time state office, his assets were
$2,000 in pledges. In the end we spent a total of $18,000
on the five major candidates' campaigns.

We used our own or borrowed cars to travel around the
state. We stayed in private houses, and ate with friends
as often as possible. The election was in September, so
the bulk of the campaign took place in the summer months
when most of Maine is preoccupied with the pleasures and
the business of that short season. In the beginning we didn't
get very big crowds, and I know that my repeated speeches
about two-party government didn't stir much excitement
among the more partisan Democrats. But I was able to
point out and drum home the argument that one-party
domination had hurt the state: The most Republican counties were the poorest counties. I was also determined not
to sound like a conventional, tub-thumping politician simply
looking for a way to get something for me and my party.
I think the turning point in the campaign came in early
August. I had called for an economic study as part of a
program to get Maine out of the doldrums. My opponent
ridiculed the proposal. And then a young college professor,
who had been combing newspaper accounts of my opponent's
career, discovered that the incumbent Republican governor
had made a similar proposal during the 1952 Republican

primary and had never followed up on it. That broke open the state's economic problems and Republican indifference as the central issue of the campaign. We pounded the theme home in town after town in the final weeks of the summer, trying without success to get the governor to debate me. The crowds built up. Our workers, including the Republicans for Muskie organization, got more and more enthusiastic. We thought we had the best campaign in years, but we really didn't think we would win. I remember a column that appeared in the Lewiston *Evening Journal* the Saturday before the election. Their political editor wrote that the Democratic campaign that had threatened to become a "tidal wave, had become just a ripple" on the surface of Maine's political waters. Much to his shock, and ours, the next Tuesday we won the governorship. It was the beginning of steady Democratic growth in the state.

Why did we win that year? The first of the Eisenhower recessions helped. An impolitic governor, who could say after viewing hurricane damage a week before the election, "It isn't as bad as I expected," gave us a big boost. But the most important ingredient may well have been that team of candidates who had nothing to gain from the campaign, but who believed in their cause, took the party's platform seriously, and were able to offer Maine voters a genuine alternative to one-party domination of the state. That was the first year television played a role in Maine campaigns, and it had a major impact on voters. For the first time, many voters discovered that Democrats could be reasonable, articulate, and concerned about the day-to-day problems that bothered them. We also used a series of five-minute radio programs to carry the same message.

In a sense we were ahead of our time, in the emphasis we placed on voter participation in the development of our platform, in the work we did to expand involvement in party organization, in our involvement of young people, and in our efforts to broaden the base of campaign contributions. Those of us who ran that campaign in 1954 were not labeled as reformers, but that was what we were. We simply did what had to be done, and we tried to establish principles that would maintain a reform process in the party. The Maine Democratic Party is not a perfect instrument, but it continues to be a remarkable combination of youth and age, receptive to new ideas and new workers, and oriented to issues as the foundation of responsive and responsible politics.

I realize that reform and change are harder in larger states, where the structure has been rigid for much longer periods of time than we experienced in Maine, but I think reform can be accomplished in other states, not in intermittent bursts, but as a continuing process. The reforms approved by the Democratic National Committee are a good first step, although more needs to be done.

The biggest reform requirements in politics today are in the areas of fund-raising and expenditures. The costs of campaigning have grown immensely since I first ran for governor. In 1970, for example, my campaign organization spent nearly ten times as much in my bid for re-election as the Maine Democratic Party spent in the entire campaign for the five major candidates in 1954. The prospects for the 1972 presidential race are even more horrendous.

The cost of elections and the way in which they are financed generate tremendous pressures in the direction of corruption of the whole political process. That it hasn't been more corrupt is something of a political surprise. It is a dangerous situation. There are tens of thousands of campaigns for federal, state, and local offices every election year. On what basis do you publicly fund all the races? We don't yet have the best means worked out, either to cut the costs or to reduce the dependence on relatively small numbers of large contributors.

Some have suggested putting arbitrary limits on the length of campaigns, but if you did that you would tend to support incumbents against challengers. Incumbents always benefit by a short campaign; challengers usually need a longer campaign. And so, to the extent that you limit the length of election contests, you protect those who already have office. That's not helpful.

There are certain things that we should do to reduce the pressures for high expenditures, to encourage small gifts, and to impose public controls on such activities as television advertising. There are ways of getting at the problem, and I think the legislation the Congress enacted in 1972 is a sensible beginning. By dealing with the presidency first of all, it deals with the office that above all others should be free of corruption. By restricting television costs, the new law gets at the most explosive costs, and that's good. By offering tax credits, it makes a step in the direction of inviting the average citizen to get involved in campaign financing, and to get away from the big contributor. The disclosure provisions get contributions more on the record.

Under existing circumstances, campaign managers and fundraisers depend too much on the big givers. The smaller contributors are harder to reach, and the biggest contributions return far more to the campaign for the amount of solicitation effort involved. The campaign financial managers tend to approach the big givers because it takes fewer of them, the job is easier, they are more accustomed to it, and they understand it.

Big contributions lead inevitably to questions of private

versus public interest. A surprising number of those contributors are not looking for anything in return for their gifts,
but the economic stakes of public policy are high enough
to raise clouds of suspicion. I have encountered almost no
direct evidence of *quid pro quos* for campaign contributions.
That is no argument against the possibility, however, and we
do not have to unearth venal arrangements to uncover the
real dangers in campaign finance.

There are sectors of our economic life in America that
are more dependent upon government policies, government
appropriations, government programs, and government activities than others. To protect their interest they don't need
a direct commitment from candidates; they know that this is
a pretty risky course to follow. I doubt that there is very
much of that, although I may be naive on that point because
I haven't been offered that kind of contribution.

It isn't the direct *quid pro quo* that is important; that isn't
the vulnerable part of this whole business. The special-in-
terest contributors don't need that. They can follow the voting
records of senators and congressmen. For example, people
in the defense industries know that certain senators or congressmen are hawkish in their view of their country's security
requirements. The contributors don't need a direct understanding, or even an implied one. They're not buying anything. They just support those candidates because they have
a shared interest in that point of view. They are willing to
make the contributions and the people whose campaigns they
support may not even stop to think about the question of
interests.

The underlying question is one of equality. We are in
the process of broadening the franchise and of insuring
"one man, one vote" in every aspect of electoral politics.
But so long as some people, because of their wealth, can

influence the ability of candidates to mount effective campaigns, some voters are in fact more equal than others. That inequality must be erased if the other reforms are to have any meaning.

Reducing candidate dependence on a small group of contributors can't be done with one law, or with a one-shot reform effort. We should have learned from the history of the Corrupt Practices Act that the reform process has to continue and to adapt to new conditions. Campaign techniques change, including methods of organization and finance. Not all the possible techniques can be foreseen, and campaign organizers are, of necessity, ingenious in seeking out ways to gain advantages. That should not discourage us, but it ought to remind us that keeping the democratic system clean and fair is not a job for the "summer soldier."

Most politicians are amateur political scientists. From time to time we try to spell out the principles that guide us, and we even try to understand the rules of political behavior by which we ply our trade. Unfortunately for our perspective, and fortunately for those who write political science textbooks, our time for rumination and writing is restricted by the press of daily events. Once in a while, however, a political figure distills a bit of political philosophy that ought to be remembered.

When I was governor of the state of Maine, my press secretary's wife, Mrs. Alice Nute, who is a state librarian, collected and gave me two bound volumes of the inaugural addresses of all the Maine governors. It was a thoughtful gift, and a useful one. I felt a kinship with the governors who preceded me, and who had struggled with some of the same problems I faced, some more than one hundred years earlier. I dipped into those two volumes on more than one occasion, and in the course of my reading I found the following lines in the fourth inaugural address of Governor Joshua Chamberlain (Maine governors had one-year terms at the time):

A government has something more to do than to govern, and levy taxes to pay the governors. It is something more than a policy to arrest evil and punish wrong. It must also encourage good, point out improvements, open roads of prosperity and infuse life into all right enterprises. It should combine the insight and foresight of the best minds of the state for all the high ends for which society is established and to which man aspires.

That gives us much to do.

Governor Chamberlain was a Civil War general, sometimes called the "hero of Little Round Top" because of his leadership of the 20th Marine Regiment at the Battle of Gettysburg. He came home after the war to a state that had lost many young men in that conflict and was losing many more to the rich and easily harvested lands of the Midwest. He was a Republican and he was governor from 1867 to 1870. He was one of the most progressive governors in our state's history, and I like to think he would have been a Democrat today.

Governor Chamberlain spoke, as I think any humane politician must, to the obligation of government to serve the people of our society. At a time when government is in disrepute and politicians are held in contempt it is easy to look on our political institutions as alien powers that should be kept as impotent as possible. I can't accept that view, not because I am a political practitioner, but because I believe that the absence of responsive and responsible government can only lead to one or another form of tyranny.

There is a myth some of our politicians like to keep alive, that the men who drafted the Constitution wanted to keep government as weak as possible. The fact is that the Constitutional Convention of 1787 came together to deal with the problem of the Articles of Confederation which had provided a government so weak as to be almost no government at all. They aimed at a government that would be effective without destroying individual liberty. It had its checks and balances, but it was meant to work. They were not as careful of civil liberties as many had hoped, and the result was the Bill of Rights which became the condition for adoption of the new Constitution.

When I am discouraged at the prospects for uniting our country and making our democracy work I remember the trials that the founding fathers went through even after the new Constitution was ratified and the government was formed. The Bill of Rights was aimed at individual liberty, but for George Washington, John Adams, and others, freedom of speech and assembly did not confer a right to disrupt the government by factions—and by factions they meant political parties. They had watched the corrupt parties of England, and they wanted to avoid their excesses here. In addition, the sense of identification between the emerging Jeffersonian Democratic-Republican Party and the revolutionaries of France terrified these leaders who wanted stability in the infant republic. We got the Alien and Sedition laws as a result, but before long the party system developed as a healthy part of our democracy.

Parties are not perfect, any more than individual citizens or political leaders are perfect, but they are remarkable instruments for giving individuals a chance to join their voices and to apply their combined wills to social and economic problems. The answer to venal, unresponsive, or repressive government or parties is not to end them, but to improve them, and the only way I know how to do that is to work at it. My own career in politics has been one of laboring to improve what I found, and for me the approach has worked, not so much as a benefit for me—although I have found great satisfactions in my work—but as a reaffirmation of the faith in democracy that my father instilled in me. And I have found this to be so at practically every stage of my career.

In my two terms as governor I faced Republican majorities in the House and the Senate. The winds of change were strong enough to get me elected, but they were not yet strong enough to sweep aside the string of Republican legislatures that had been broken only once since the Civil War. With a small staff, supplemented by volunteers, and with the benefit of a receptive citizenry, I set out to make some needed changes in state government. The cards were stacked against me, and not just by the legislative majority. Maine's constitution had been written in 1820 as if governors were still King George III's appointees. An executive council, elected by the majority party in the legislature, is a permanent legislative watchdog on the governor. It advises and consents on gubernatorial appointments; it advises the governor on pardons; and its approval is required for many financial transactions involving the governor. Only Maine, Massachusetts, and New Hampshire retain that vestige from colonial days. There was, furthermore, no cabinet as such. Department heads were appointed for fixed terms not contiguous with the governor's two-year term. In order to govern, the governor had to use all his persuasive and political skills.

My biggest task was to meet state needs in education,

mental health, and corrective institutions, and economic development. Through the fall of 1954, after our September elections, I divided my time between campaign trips for Democrats in other states and budget hearings in Augusta. I soon found that the state's needs far exceeded our tax revenues. I also found that the governor had very limited control over departmental budgets and expenditures. The legislature appropriated what amounted to lump sums for the departments to spend in the biennium. Department heads had considerable flexibility in the transfer of funds within their agencies, and toward the end of each fiscal year there was a great scramble to spend what money was left in the till. This practice, coupled with the budget office's habit of overestimating expenditures and underestimating revenues, gave the illusion of fiscal health, while in fact the state was suffering because sufficient funds were not being expended for what Governor Chamberlain had called "the high ends for which society is established and to which man aspires."

With the aid of my administrative assistant Maurice Williams, who had been the assistant budget officer for the state, I moved to tighten up revenue and expenditure estimates. I allocated surplus funds for capital expenditures, instituted an effective line budget, under which department heads were forced to spend only for budgeted items, and presented the legislature with a two-part budget: Part I related to current services and Part II included proposed new services. Part I was to be financed out of current revenues and Part II would be financed out of new taxes. The Republicans had hoped that I would submit an unbalanced budget that would enable them to tag me with their traditional Democratic "tax and spend" label. I was determined that the voters should know what current services were costing them and understand clearly what unmet needs had to be financed out of higher taxes. I was convinced that Maine citizens would support an approach that was fiscally sound and responsive to the state's needs. They did and as a result we were able to enact 65 per cent of our program in that legislature.

As I talked with other governors, I learned that we shared similar problems and that the sizes of our states and our regions made only superficial differences in the aspirations of our citizens. I also learned that governors, acting together, could be a powerful force for change in our national government. It is a curious thing that the governors, as a group, have exerted more influence on national policies during a period when their individual standings as independent, national political figures have declined. There are some who would say that the reverse is true of United States senators.

At times, I think, people wonder what happens at Governors Conferences, or if anything does. Actually, as I have noted, over the years the governors have exerted a healthy influence on the federal government in a number of policy areas.

In the 1950s, when I was a member of the Conference, the governors made a plea for a share of the federal government's revenues, pressing the government to give up a two-cent gasoline tax and let the states impose and collect it. There was a continual pressure exerted for a share of federal revenues, or, as many governors saw it, for the recovery of revenue the federal government had pre-empted. They felt they needed to do this in order to strengthen the fiscal base of the states.

The Eisenhower administration's approach to this was typical of what we have encountered during the past three years, too little and too late. First, the President proposed to the Governors Conference at Williamsburg, Virginia, in 1957, to create a task force of governors and cabinet members to explore sources of revenue that might be returned to the states and programs that could be turned over at the same time. The task force eventually recommended turning over to the states part of the federal excise tax on telephone messages. In return the states would accept responsibility for the new waste-treatment program and others, including a vocational education plan. About $100 million in program costs would be required of the states while they would pick up about $150 million in revenues. In other words, they would have a "profit" of $50 million.

On the face of it, this looked good. I was on the Executive Committee of the Governors Conference and we had a meeting in Little Rock, Arkansas, to study the proposal and to develop a recommendation for the Conference. In the process of analyzing it, I discovered that the states which would get the bulk of tax revenues were the states which were already rather well off—California and New York, for example—and the states which would take on the bulk of the program costs would be those whose needs were the greatest. It was hardly a good bargain for all states.

At about midnight, on the evening before the Executive Committee was to meet, I roughed out what the program would cost each of the governors who were present at the meeting. The session the next morning was amusing. As the proposal was discussed, the reactions were positive. There were southern governors present and it all looked like a states' rights position. The whole mood was positive. Then I said, "Well, before we go much further, I'd like to give you some figures." When I revealed the net results of the proposition, the meeting turned around, and the proposal was dead from that moment on. It never got off the ground because it was obvious that the needs of the states and the revenues involved were in inverse proportion. When the federal government gives up a tax source, instead of distributing funds under a population and need formula, it almost inevitably benefits the richer states more than the poorer states.

None of which meant that I was against either treatment programs or vocational education. The episode was simply an indication that you had to use a sharp pencil to treat with problems of waste and disposal as well as with problems of the Republican administration's revenue disposal.

Revenue sharing is, among other things, an attempt to give new life to state and local governments. Most of us are convinced that a democratic society is healthiest when a maximum number of decisions can be made close to home. But if schools are in disrepair and there aren't enough teachers, if police can't keep up with muggings and burglaries, if mental institutions are jails and jails are schools for crime, if the garbage isn't collected, and if public transportation has collapsed, voters have a right to be cynical about the value of state and local jurisdictions. I do not believe we can afford to let state and local governments collapse under the weight of public needs that far exceed their resources. It is not that those governments are now more virtuous than the federal government; nor is it a question of relative talent. The national government simply cannot respond as immediately or as well to a local need as the local agencies—if those agencies have adequate resources, and if they must meet basic standards of equality and fairness.

So much of our lives is taken up in impersonal associations. Entertainment comes in an electronic box. Vegetables are prewrapped in plastic. Our mail is routed by zip code, and we are now considering the proposal to give children Social Security card numbers. We charge by plastic card, are billed by computers, and pay by check. In many places the vending machine has replaced the salesclerk, and it's not easy to communicate with a vending machine that doesn't work.

We can't go back to the simpler life that I knew, or that my parents knew. There are too many people, and too many things have happened for us to be able to re-create the small-town, personal life that occupies so much of our nostalgia. And I know there are millions of Americans who want no part of that nostalgic, simpler life. They have fled the small towns and the rural farms to seek new opportunities in the cities and metropolitan areas. Our restless, mobile population has covered more towns and smothered the boundaries that once made them separate communities. The bigger and better houses, and the more efficient and sophisticated appliances of suburban housing developments spell "progress" for many, but the price of such material advancement has been a loss of that sense of community which is so essential to a healthy democracy. That is a loss that cannot be corrected by the supply of a few more federal dollars to make sure the highway system keeps pace with the flow of automobile traffic, or that the garbage and the trash are collected on time.

The two major institutional problems facing metropolitan areas are regional co-operation and responsive local government. We have aimed to correct the first with regional planning grants and the encouragement of such agencies as metropolitan councils of government. The second is more difficult because it is so intertwined with the physical focus of a local jurisdiction, its history, and that sense of identity that can only come with the experience of working together. None of these ingredients can be manufactured overnight, and only the last is susceptible to the quality of political leadership.

In our preoccupation with international policy and with national campaigns, we tend to forget that the strength of the country depends heavily on the social and economic health of thousands of communities, where the lessons of mutual confidence and co-operation are learned or forgotten. These are the laboratories where experiments in national policy are tried, and where successes or failures are enjoyed or suffered. These are the places where such concepts as equality and justice are tested to see if they have meaning in the classrooms and the job markets, on the streets, and in the courthouses. If democracy doesn't work in the community, it won't work at our national conventions or in our national capital, and if our communities are not whole, then the United States cannot fulfill its national responsibilities at home or abroad.

CHAPTER VIII

●

Toward New Perspectives

FOR THOSE of us who reached our majority in the 1930s, particularly in the mill towns of Maine, the economic shadow of the Depression was our constant companion. But the memories and threats of world conflict were only slightly less important to us. I remember that my high school valedictory speech (1932) was keyed to the Kellogg-Briand Pact, the treaty that was to end all war. And all the while we worried about peace and our domestic economy pressures were building in Europe and in Asia that would engulf all of us. I had barely established my law practice when the Japanese attacked Pearl Harbor.

The war took me out of the continental United States for the first time, but it did not give me much of a view of the world. A new perspective would have to wait until my service in the Senate.

There were a few opportunities for travel and meetings overseas between the time I entered the Senate and 1970, but they were limited by the fact that I was not a member of the Senate Committee on Foreign Relations. My legislative responsibilities concentrated my attention on domestic problems.

Throughout that period the world was changing, my views of the world were changing, and there was a chance that one day I might have work to do that was global, as well as local and national. Early in 1970, I decided that the time had come to plan some new journeys.

The fall disappeared without any chance for me to make a single trip. The only open time was between Christmas and January 21, when Congress would convene again. So I decided to get going.

We worked out a program that would take me to Europe, the Middle East, and the Soviet Union. My objective was to travel only to countries that were interested in having us and would offer substantial talks with their leaders. I was not interested in tourism or ceremonial visits or even courtesy calls. In the case of the Russians, there had been tentative inquiries from their direction, through several sources. There had been inquiries also by Governor Averell Harriman and others, and from Georgi Arbatov, head of the U.S.A. Studies Institute, which is part of the Soviet Academy of Sciences.

The Soviets were the last to give us a firm indication that I could meet with their leaders. This is typical, of course; they didn't commit themselves any sooner than they had to (although, others might say, perhaps I should be the last one to remark on this). The final commitment was made at lunch at the Soviet Embassy where Ambassador Dobrynin and I were together for about three hours. The meeting was friendly, even though, on the day before, I had cosponsored a resolution which in effect condemned the Soviet Union for its treatment of Jews and for the Leningrad Trial. The Ambassador denied that there was anti-Semitism in the Soviet Union. He used about the same arguments that Mr. Kosygin would later use when I raised the issue of Soviet treatment of Jews. There was nothing in his attitude to indicate that leniency was being considered, but the next day the Soviets announced a reduction of the sentences.

At the end of our long conversation he said, "I'm authorized to tell you that you will meet with Mr. Kosygin or Mr. Brezhnev, or both."

I asked if he had any objections to Averell Harriman accompanying me. He said, "Of course not."

It made sense to ask Averell to join me in Moscow. The Governor is an old Russian hand, going back to the early twenties. He is respected in the Soviet Union, and I knew that his advice could be vital to me at some point. He was delighted to go. As it happened, he decided to take his two granddaughters with him.

Our journey took us to Israel, Egypt, the Soviet Union, and Germany. The latter two countries I had visited before, but I had never been to Israel or Egypt.

I had wanted to go to Israel for a long time, and when I arrived I felt a sense of having been there before. Much of the travel through Israel was, for me, like a journey through the Bible. The Israelis have done much to transform what was a poor and depleted country into a vigorous and productive land, but they have also preserved much that is part of our hallowed traditions. My principal business was the talks with Prime Minister Meir, Deputy Premier Alon, Foreign Minister Eban, Defense Minister Dayan, Finance Minister Sapir, and other public and private leaders. Those conversations were enhanced by the experience of seeing their land and their people. I saw better than I ever could on paper or in State Department reports what Israel is really all about. When I stood in Yad Vashem, the memorial to the six million Jews martyred by the Nazis, I remembered my father's explanation of America's meaning to him—to a man who found in Rumford, Maine, a decent refuge from the oppression of Eastern Europe. The kind of life he built there and the kind of life Jews have built in Israel are things too precious to lose.

In Jerusalem we stayed one night at the King David Hotel, had breakfast with Mayor Kollek, walked through the Old City with him, visited the Shrine of the Book, saw the Church of the Holy Sepulchre, visited the Dome of the Rock (the Moslem shrine containing the rock on which, according to tradition, Abraham almost sacrificed his son). We visited the Wailing Wall, of course. I hadn't been able to visualize the extent to which Judaism, Mohammedanism, and Christianity had their origins in that city. The Church of the Holy Sepulchre is in the process of restoration. This can be accomplished only with the agreement of different religious orders. Each is interested in preserving elements important to his own traditions, while not violating the others. And they are doing it. This renewal of the ancient traditions may hold out hope of working out modern differences elsewhere. Reconstruction is a slow process but it goes on, containing a promise of the future.

In some ways the most memorable experience for me was the hour I spent with one of the great men of the twentieth century, David Ben-Gurion. He lives in a simple cottage on a kibbutz in the Negev. He is surrounded by the desert and is guarded by troops and barbed wire, but he lives as a free spirit in the midst of his memories and the young people

who share his immediate concerns for the life and future of
Israel. Ben-Gurion talked with me of many things, from the
perspective of a warm and vibrant man who is still living a
full and productive life. But the most moving things he
said to me—and the ones which will remain with me—
were his comments about Judaism. He said Judaism can be
summarized in three sentences: There is one God. Love
thy neighbor as thyself. Love the truth and peace.

His words stayed with me as we flew from the Negev
north toward Galilee, over Herod's summer palace at Mes-
sada, across the hills of Judea, past Bethlehem and Jerusalem, west of the Jordan River to Belvoir, the site of an old
crusader fort, where we landed. From there we drove down
toward the Sea of Galilee, now called Kinneret.

Near the shore of Kinneret we visited a kibbutz, and
talked with its members over lunch and in a tour of their
living quarters and their communal facilities. I was struck by
the healthy, cohesive attitude of the members, happy in spite
of the pressures under which they live. Here, in the shadow
of the Golan Heights, from which they were bombarded
over the years, they had built bomb shelters, for their children
especially. As we lunched, one of the young fathers said that
what concerned them most was that their children would
grow up learning hatred of their neighbors. They were trying to avoid that in their nursery shelters; they had painted
on the walls the symbols of peace—birds, trees. No propaganda. No war.

In a new kibbutz being built by young Israelis on the
Golan Heights I asked what they did with their leisure
time. They said there was another kibbutz on the shores of
Kinneret, below, and they went there to concerts and to the
library. Over and over again I was inspired by their devotion
to the pursuits of peace and by their idealism. I am con-

vinced that the Israelis are effective militarily because they fight not as professional soldiers but for a way of life. No one could have taken those Heights and sustained the losses they did unless they were moved by something other than the love of war.

This is why they will not give up the Heights. As we talked, one man said, "Well now, Senator, you've been here to Golan Heights . . . What do you think of our claim to them?"

I was extremely conscious of the fact that we were going to Egypt next and didn't want to create diplomatic problems—not in the sense of any personal discomfort for me but problems that would preclude meaningful talks in Egypt. Nevertheless, it seemed to me that this was a good place to make a point that I would use later in Egypt and then in the Soviet Union. "If I were in your shoes," I said, "I'd hold on to them." I did not think, and I do not believe, that anyone can deal with the problem of borders and security between Israel and her Arab neighbors without understanding the relationship between the Golan Heights and the threatened kibbutzim on the shores of Kinneret.

When I did get to Egypt, the question was raised—not by the Egyptian leaders but by Walter Cronkite. He had been there to tape a program with President Sadat and he thought that I'd pulled a real boner in making such a statement just before coming to Egypt. At a little cocktail party, when Egyptian businessmen came in to the consulate in Cairo to talk, several Egyptian newsmen asked for an explanation. I gave them essentially the same explanation given here, and they did not press the point. But President Sadat, the Foreign Minister of Egypt, Premier Kosygin, and Foreign Minister Gromyko never raised it.

A conversation with Golda Meir was important to me.

We had met before at a dinner, shortly after she became
Prime Minister. As the ranking American there, I had the
good fortune to be her table companion throughout. She is
very comfortable. Some people see her as grandmotherly. I
see in her the qualities that the leader of a country ought to
have. Her "comfortableness" is part of her humanity, but it
does not interfere with her capacity to make hard decisions.

In our Jerusalem conversation she spoke of her responsibilities and of the problems of peace. What was important, so
far as she was concerned, was the quality of the peace that
might come out of a basic settlement, rather than the particular details of territorial adjustments. To give this emphasis, she said this at the start of our talk. If she had said it
a half hour later, it would not have made the same impression.

Mrs. Meir encouraged me to bring up the question of the
Russian Jews when I arrived in Moscow. She knew my
itinerary and she said she hoped I would have the opportunity to challenge the Soviet treatment of the Jews. Obviously, she felt deeply about this. She knew that I was not
carrying messages. She believed that this point had to be
made whenever possible by people visiting the Soviet Union
who might have any influence at all. I promised her that I
would.

When we met President Sadat of Egypt, in his home on
the Barrages of the Nile, he entered the room, we shook
hands and sat down on the couch together. He looked at me,
smiled, and said, "My, you're very young. I should think you
are too young to expect to be President of the United
States."

"Well, Mr. President," I said, "I suspect that you are
younger than I."

He expressed doubt about that and so we compared ages. He was about three or four years my junior. The next morning Mohamed Heikal, editor of the Cairo newspaper *Al Ahram,* told me that this dialogue had created a slight problem in the Sadat household. After we left, Mrs. Sadat twitted her husband about being younger but looking older than I.

Our conversation ranged over the problems affecting relations between the United States and Egypt and the prospects for peace between the Arab states and Israel. I was impressed by several facets of that conversation. First, President Sadat was acutely conscious of the economic and social needs of his country, and he understood that he needed peace in order to meet those needs. At the same time, the history of foreign domination in Egypt and the Israeli occupation of Egyptian territory had generated powerful obstacles to a peaceful settlement. I made no secret of my conviction that Israeli security had to be a principal concern for the United States, but I also made it clear that the people of the United States wanted to contribute to a restoration of normal relations between their country and Egypt with the achievement of peace in the Middle East. I expressed concern at Soviet military involvement, but I believed then as I do now that we should not contribute to a cold-war atmosphere in the Middle East. Neither do I believe that we should try to shape a settlement between the Israelis and the Arabs. The only peace that will be worth anything must be worked out between those directly concerned.

As our party flew toward the Soviet Union, I thought back to an earlier time, 1959, and to an earlier visit. It was my first year in the Senate, and a time in which I looked on the world with a different perspective. The changes in our political system and outlook were, perhaps, concurrent with such changes elsewhere in the world. I have confessed to the state of mind in which I, and others like me, graduated from high school, not oblivious to the world but certainly unrealistic about what sort of leaders and events influenced nations. The terrible series of shocks, of Hitler, Mussolini, and Japan, which led to that collective effort called World War II, had swept us out of our shells. It was not just isolationists who had been isolated; it was all of us who somehow thought that there was the United States and then the rest of the world, as a sort of large suburb.

I had, however, one distinct link to the "other" or outer world: my ancestry. So, near the end of the fifties, when an opportunity arose to see for myself the peoples and lands of Eastern Europe and the U.S.S.R., I took it, gladly.

The trip originated in the Interior Committee with an opportunity to study the hydroelectric system in the Soviet Union. Senator Frank Moss (D-Utah) and Senator Ernest Gruening (D-Alaska) first approached me in August about going on the trip in September, which was short notice, but I quickly agreed.

This was at the time of Khrushchev's visit to the United States. He would have taken it as no affront, had he known, but at about the time he was landing in Washington, I was taking off for Moscow. We spent almost a week in that city, not studying hydroelectric power but contending with bureaucratic power, trying to obtain agreement for an itinerary which we thought had been agreed to before we left home. We kept making calls back to the State Department, in order to get support for as broad an itinerary as possible. The Russians were interested in negotiating everything *quid pro quo*. It would not have done any good to tell them they could see anything they wanted in our country. We had to go through the process of bargaining. If they let us go to one place, they wanted an agreement to go to a place in the United States—so we had to act as though everything was a question of negotiation. Ultimately, we visited Moscow, Leningrad, Stalingrad, Kuybyshev, Tbilisi, Rostov, and in Siberia, Lake Baikal and a large development at Bratsk near Irkutsk.

We traveled some twelve thousand miles, taking almost thirty days. The Russians had made real progress in hydroelectricity. We took the opportunity to study other aspects of Russian life, including the collective farms, the state farms, and to a limited extent Russian homes, Russian construction, and schools.

At times we were conscious of an oppressive or repressive atmosphere in the Soviet Union. But so far as the citizens of Russia were concerned we got nothing but friendly response everywhere we went. When we went walking on the streets, people looked at us with curiosity, but they were polite. Once, several Russian students stopped us, to say that they had been studying English and they wanted to practice on us. As soon as that happened, a crowd gathered, all of them friendly. The Russian and English flowed like vodka, a little drunkenly. The atmosphere of the countryside was different, too, than that of the cities. That is not uniquely Soviet; cities are more impersonal, whether in the Soviet Union or elsewhere.

At Leningrad, I left the rest of the party, who were going down the Dnepr River to visit the hydroelectric developments there. I was on my way to Poland. I wanted to go "back"—though I had never been there before. To see the home of my father, his original home, at any rate, would be, in a sense, going home, too. There was a picture of the village in my mind.

I had a reservation on a Soviet commercial flight from Leningrad to Moscow, where I was to get the plane to

Warsaw. The plane was scheduled to leave at 7:30 or 8 P.M., but when I got on board, the departure was delayed. I seemed to be the only American and, as far as I could tell, the only English-speaking person on the plane. Repeatedly, the hostess made announcements that I could not understand. I sat there thinking that eventually something would happen and I would know when we were going.

It had been a long thirty days and I was so tired that sitting there I fell asleep. When I awoke, the plane was in darkness. There was no one on it. I looked around; we still seemed to be in Leningrad. Outside, there was no sign of activity. I looked at my watch—2 A.M. When I went into the airport, I could find no one at the counter who spoke English. People working around the place were obviously trying to be help-ful, but I was getting no answers I could understand. Even-tually, I managed to phone the hotel to get in touch with the rest of my party. As luck would have it, they were on their way to the airport—to take their flight to Moscow. So, even-tually, I ended up on that plane back to Moscow, but I had had an uncertain moment. I remember being impressed with the Soviets' sense of self-sufficiency. If you couldn't under-stand announcements in Russian, presumably you weren't worth bothering about when a plane was evacuated. That plane had emptied out, whatever the reason for the delay, leaving me there, with nobody concerned about it. I might still be there.

When we landed in Warsaw, any feeling of repression, of mystery, faded. It was not just imaginary, I think; there was a visible difference in people. It was so real as to be tangible. Here were people who had known freedom, at least. You sensed that they did, even though they were worse off economically by far than the Russians and were living under a government not necessarily of their own choosing.

At about that time stories were running in the press about what some people regarded as a miracle, a divine visitation in Poland. There was a church in Warsaw where the apparition or vision was said to have occurred at the top of the steeple. People were convinced that this was a sign from God. When I saw the church, they were walking around it, thousands of them, placing lighted candles on the sidewalk. It was a tremendous outpouring of response to what seemed to be a message from the divine.

The Poles, very religious people, had been allowed to continue the practice of their religion. Roadside shrines all over Poland were well kept and obviously used. That Sunday the churches were full.

On the first day, the Embassy car drove me west to Poznan, the site of massacres in the 1950s, when residents rioted against the government. Along the way, at my request, we went off the main road to visit the ancient Polish capital of Gniezno, a lovely little town, and went to Mass there in the old cathedral. It was a beautiful fall day and a lovely drive. Poznan had been the eastern outpost of Bismarck's empire. We visited the burial ground of the victims of the massacres, on the site of a fortification that Bismarck had built. It was one of the anchors of the eastern line. No longer used as a fortification, its bricks were slowly being taken out to be used for construction. Building materials were scarce, and the Poles were smashing the old outpost, using it to reconstruct the downtown area. They were reconstructing historical buildings, too, destroyed in the bombing of World War II. An ancient cathedral where the first Polish kings were buried had been completely redone, and beautifully. There was a local town hall, an ancient building, fully restored. The sentiment for preservation is still there and their religious freedom was part of the agreeable atmosphere. Another part of it was style. Women dressed with a Western flair that you didn't see elsewhere in the Communist world. They made attractive use of cosmetics and hair styling.

We went on then, headed for the real goal, my father's village. I had seen it in my mind's eye, and when you have the sense that you are approaching a place identified with your past, a place which often has been described to you, there is an emotional sweep to it all. First, the countryside was lovely. The next thing I noticed, to my pleasure, was a lake, named, nicely enough, Lake Augusta. My father had never mentioned the lake but the fact that this was also the name of the capital of our state was a welcome coincidence. Soon, as we approached the village, we came upon a farm and it made me think of the farm he had described, which his father managed, and where he spent his boyhood. It turned out that this was the farm, now managed by the state.

In the village stood a church, and I remembered it now, his descriptions of it, and how he spoke of his father's relationship with the priest. They had more than a few flaming arguments about the proper sphere for a priest to exercise his authority, and the proper sphere for my grandfather to exercise his judgment. It was one of the early debates in my family on the separation of church and state, I suppose. My grandfather and the priest had argued the way my father and some of his customers would argue later. Perhaps I continue this unruly tradition. I like to think of it as independence.

Only one old lady in the village still carried the family name. We went into her meager dwelling, in the poor town, in the poorest section of the country, dimly lit and sparsely furnitured. She opened the trunk and reached in and drew out some pictures my father had sent years and years before. It was a moving experience to see him there, in this way.

At the end, we went to visit the cemetery that my father used to talk about, about how frightened the kids were when walking past it at night. When we looked to see if we could find any family tombstones, we found just one with the name on it. It was on its side.

With those memories behind and a face-to-face meeting with one or more Russian leaders ahead, I flew to Moscow and to a happy welcome from Governor Harriman, my "advance man."

How good it was to have his counsel. He is an incredible man, and his instincts on how to move and how to operate were perfect. I wanted to talk about the Middle East problem, the SALT disarmament talks, the status of the negotiations in Berlin, and Chancellor Brandt's *Ostopolitik*. In addition, I would keep my promise to Mrs. Meir.

Premier Kosygin met me most cordially in his office, which was full of photographers. I learned later that we were on Russian television that night which was, they said, rather unprecedented. Kosygin seemed friendly, smiling, and relaxed as we began our conversation. He asked whether or not I had been to Russia before. I'm sure he knew, but I mentioned the visit in 1959. I expressed my admiration for Lake Baikal, for its beauty and unusual qualities. It is a mile deep, with an ecology unlike any other place in the world, with some species found nowhere else on earth. I said that I had learned that the Russians were building a paper mill on the shore, which disturbed me because environmentalists all over the world, including in Russia, were opposed to it.

He told me that they had taken steps to protect the waters of the lake. He expanded on his interest in environment as part of the planned development of the Soviet Union, and he was especially enthusiastic when talking about proposals to reverse the flow of some of the northern-flowing rivers in Siberia and European Russia, in order to divert the waters from the Arctic, where they are not considered particularly useful, to the more arid, unpopulated regions of southern Russia. It is a considerable engineering feat. He showed me the map and discussed the proposal in detail. I have noted, since that discussion, that a number of environmentalists doubt the wisdom of the proposed diversion.

It was interesting how many of the leaders of the countries we were visiting were more enthusiastic about discussing future development in their countries than focusing on the present facts of war, hardship, and the fate of other countries. In each instance, this seemed to be their instinct. We would expect it of the Israelis, perhaps, but it was also true of President Sadat and of the Russians.

In any event, such talk made a good opening. I built upon it to suggest how important it was that the United States and the Soviet Union find as many areas as possible in which to build not only power plants and factories but habits of co-operation. Environmental concerns, I suggested, might well be in the forefront of co-operative efforts. In his speech to the twenty-fourth Soviet Congress, Mr. Brezhnev listed environment as one of the areas of possible international co-operation. I found that my long interest and work in what was once a pressing domestic matter had become the basis for conversation in foreign policy.

Premier Kosygin obviously had been well briefed on me and on the subject. There were two things about that section of the conversation which intrigued me. First, it was the only place in the entire conversation where President Nixon's name was brought up. He said that Mr. Nixon had made the comment that Lake Baikal was filling up with silt. "I don't know where he got that piece of information," said Mr. Kosygin. "It's not true and we certainly didn't give it to him."

At the end, Mr. Kosygin raised the question of eutrophication (the destruction of a body of water through excessive plant growth) behind the dams on their major power projects. He said he understood that United States scientists have been doing quite a bit of work on the problem of eutrophication and he was much interested in what they might have found. This was an obvious lead for me to talk about our need to reduce the burden of arms and the escalating cost of arms. I understood in advance that he was concerned about it, too.

I made the point that it was in the nature of things that great power generates fear rather than love and understanding. Since each of us had the power to destroy the other, we had to expect that would be the reaction on the other side. To offset it we had to take positive steps to break through the walls of fear and misunderstanding. The cost of arms had the effect of intensifying those fears, inhibiting the breakthroughs and, in addition, diverting resources, not only from the needs of each of our own people but from the important tasks of meeting the needs of backward and disadvantaged people all over the planet. We were in danger of evading the responsibility of stabilizing conditions which themselves could lead to violence and to war. In both respects, in the escalation of anxiety between the great powers and in the neglect of the human needs of others, escalating arms have the effect of enhancing the possibilities of war rather than bringing real security to either side.

I felt it was important to him to know that there was a strong body of opinion in America that felt that way about the ceaseless pursuit of armaments. For this reason it was appropriate for the two countries to spell out areas of agreement wherever we could find them. Our countries were holding formal talks with each other in at least three situations which held the possibilities to help avoid war: the Middle East, SALT, and Berlin. I said that it was important that each side exert a maximum effort to achieve meaningful agreements out of those talks.

From there, we got on to a discussion of the Middle East and related issues. I said that in addition to arms escalation, other developments in each country, from time to time, tended to raise doubts about the motives and purposes of the other side. The Jewish question in the Soviet Union was one such issue. Another development that aroused much concern in our country was the persistent report that the hardliners were taking over in the Kremlin.

He denied both, of course, and listed several Jews who held prominent positions in the Soviet Union. In order to soften my criticism of the Russians and their treatment of the Jews, I thought I would admit our own vulnerability on the problem of equality of opportunity for Blacks. I said that while we had written many laws to give Blacks legal equality, they hadn't yet achieved full economic or social equality. We could argue that this problem didn't exist by listing the names of prominent Blacks who have achieved success or eminence in the United States, I said, but that would hardly eliminate the problem.

This was the one point in the conversation when Mr. Kosygin showed some emotion. He said he resented my comparing the Jewish problem in the Soviet Union with the Black problem in the United States. We debated the question, without coming to an agreement, and without my conceding his assertion that there was no Jewish problem in the Soviet Union.

Governor Harriman and I met also with Foreign Minister Gromyko. We spent a lot of time on the question of Israel's security requirements. The Russians had supported without qualification Egypt's position on the question of territories and boundaries. We talked about withdrawal as being essential to a settlement. I felt it was important to emphasize Israel's need for some territorial or boundary adjustments in the interest of her real security needs. I was persuaded of them myself, and thought perhaps that if I emphasized this it might give the Russians a useful perspective on some American attitudes. But the talk was constantly cast by Mr. Gromyko in the context of withdrawal: Israel must agree to withdraw; Israel is really the instrument of international Zionism, and international Zionism is expansionist; this is the threat we must meet.

Finally I put it to Mr. Gromyko: We weren't really talking about withdrawal as a principle because that was not the issue the Israelis had raised; the question was what must they withdraw *to*. Suppose Israel was to agree to a substantial withdrawal and that what was left was the remainder which Israel regarded as essential to her security, at least her local security? Would the Russians then look favorably upon a resumption of the war by Egypt over that remainder? What we were talking about, I said, was rectification in terms of very genuinely felt security needs by Israel. "I've been to a couple of these places and understand their needs," I said. "What we're talking about is rectification of borders." I reminded the Foreign Minister of the border "rectification" between the Soviet Union and Finland after the Finnish war in 1940. I also reminded him of the recent agreement setting the Polish-German border along the Oder-Neisse line, also a result of World War II. Mr. Gromyko did not undertake to rebut that. The discussion was to end soon afterward.

I was interested in making that point very plain. Up to now it hasn't had much effect. As a matter of fact, our own government appeared to be willing last year to throw the point away, in the pressures it brought on Israel.

The conversation with Mr. Gromyko might have continued despite the fact that we were getting into deep Middle Eastern waters, except for the fact that our party was at the ballet and we were supposed to be with them. So we expressed our regrets, took our leave, and joined them for the final ten minutes—which is no way to attend the Bolshoi.

Upon Governor Harriman's advice, I had insisted in advance upon a stipulation with the United States ambassador about notes that were taken of my conversations with Gromyko and Kosygin.

The Governor suggested that I consider those notes my property to be used at my discretion and not to be sent routinely back to Washington by diplomatic channels. The objective was not to withhold the substance of the talks from our government but rather to make sure that they were communicated in my own way, at my own time, and in context rather than piecemeal or abbreviated. The ambassador accepted this stipulation and so did Mr. Polansky, the man from the Embassy who went along to take notes.

I learned later that the White House had asked the ambassador for a transcript. The ambassador sent back word of our agreement. The White House then ordered him to send back the notes, which he did. I found out about this through the Jack Anderson column.

When I came back home I had a meeting with Secretary of State Rogers, in which I was prepared to go into these meetings in detail. But his interest did not seem to be of a very high order.

From the beginning, in Israel and Egypt, I took the position that I would not disclose the substance of our discussions and certainly not the specific responses or the comments of the other parties to these discussions. Having adopted that as a policy, I felt we were more likely to have meaningful and frank talks. I would not want even in these reminiscences to try to characterize and certainly not to attempt to quote in detail what the other participants said.

Jane had her own schedule. She and Mrs. Donald Nicoll, Mrs. Mary Hoyt, and Governor Harriman's granddaughters visited a Russian school. The students and teachers showed expressed pleasure at the visit. Three of the students were asked to stand and say something to Jane in English. One said, "We want peace." The others made similar declarations. Jane responded with very simple statements herself, telling them that she was the mother of five children, and the grandmother of one, and that their desire for peace was what she and her children wanted, too. At which they applauded enthusiastically.

To their surprise, the teachers had a party ready. This visit was in the morning but the teachers just walked out of their classes and began the party, serving refreshments and singing for their guests. After many marvelous Russian songs, the teachers invited our ladies to respond. Jane, Mrs. Hoyt, Mrs. Nicoll, and the two Harriman granddaughters looked at each other and said, "What do we sing?" Finally, the Harriman girls said that they knew the words to "I'm Leavin' on a Jet Plane" and the others decided to hum along.

After that, they decided that they had better memorize some good American folk songs before they essayed another visit to Russia.

I met with Chancellor Willy Brandt on the way back to the United States. I was anxious to talk with him because of his initiatives in trying to restore more normal relations between Eastern and Western Europe, and because I knew United States actions could have a serious effect on what he was trying to do. We met in the Chancellor's home in the hills near Bonn, and after the usual round of premeeting photographs, the Chancellor, Foreign Minister Scheel, Secretary of State Egon Bahr (who had been instrumental in the Berlin negotiations), Governor Harriman, and I settled down to talk. The Chancellor was under no illusion that establishing anything close to "normal" relations with the Soviets or the East Germans would be easy, but he had been encouraged. He was also working hard to lay the groundwork for a European Security Conference leading to a mutual balanced force reduction. He was very open in expressing his concern over the problems raised by Senator Mansfield's proposals to cut United States forces in Europe without waiting for an agreement with the Soviet Union. He thought such a move would make a sensible arms agreement difficult to achieve, and it would make his problems in the Bundestag harder to handle.

The most immediate result of that conversation was my decision to oppose the Mansfield troop-cut amendment in 1971, even though I had supported it in the past. It brought some criticism from those who thought I was weakening on the issue of arms reduction, but I regarded it as a vote for the kind of diplomatic initiatives that had the best chance of cutting tensions and the arms race between the Western and Eastern blocs in Europe.

I was troubled during my 1971 trip, as I have been since, by the slow pace of our efforts to get control of the arms race and to stop it. There is no easy measurement of precisely how many weapons and men are enough in buying security, but I am certain that we have reached a point in history when the major powers have more than enough. The nations of the world spent $202 billion on arms in 1970. That expenditure bought us less security, not more, because the rising spiral of weapons purchases keeps upsetting the theoretical balance we were supposed to achieve at the last level. Over and over again, in United States defense requests, in the missile deployments in the Soviet Union and the United States, and in the bargaining chips built up during the SALT talks, we have seen that the threat of new weapons on one side does not convince the other side to hold off or to request a halt. It is a goad and a challenge to overmatch a new threat.

Not only are we contributing to the arms race by our strategy, we are piling up a lethal stockpile that is many times greater than what we need as a deterrent. When the current round of deployment is over, we shall have over seven thousand nuclear warheads, each several times more powerful than the bombs we dropped on Hiroshima and Nagasaki. In strategic arms alone we have the capacity to destroy our potential major enemies, and they have the capacity to destroy us. Adding to that capacity is not the way to peace or to the application of our resources to crying human needs at home and abroad.

The big powers are not alone in playing this foolish

game. The smaller countries keep adding to their "security" by the acquisition of weapons from the big suppliers. Countries that should be putting their resources in food and housing and health and education are spending most of their money on planes and guns and other weapons. They will not stop unless we stop, and the time to stop is now.

CHAPTER IX

●

Toward a World Community

IN MARCH 1971, I was able to attend the African-American dialogues in Lagos, Nigeria. The conference of African and American government and business leaders, newsmen, and scholars gave me an opportunity to see a part of the world I had not visited before, under circumstances which offered a chance to learn about the complex problems of the emerging countries from their own spokesmen.

For years, Africa had not been on the front burner of our concerns. Our foreign policy focus had been on the Soviet Union, China, the Middle East, and Southeast Asia. But Africa will be one of the most important factors in our foreign policy concerns in the next fifty years. Our preoccupation with other, more immediate questions has led us to ignore significant developments in Africa, and to sell the

Africans short, particularly when faced with pressures from such a colonial country as Portugal.

The location of the conference was of special interest. Nigeria had gone through the crucible of a civil war and was trying to bind up its wounds and cope with the rush of its rural people to the cities. Sixty million people and splendid resources give Nigeria perhaps the greatest potential for progress and economic viability of any country on the African continent.

John Lewis, a director of the Voter Education Project of the Southern Regional Council, and I were invited to make the opening American statements at the only open session of the conference. General Gowan, the head of state in Nigeria, made the first welcoming statement, and Sir Seretse Khama, President of Botswana, spoke for the African delegates to the meeting. This seemed an important opportunity to state my views of what our policy toward Africa ought to be and to make that statement in Africa.

On my way to the conference, I had been thinking of what to say. Most Americans knew, at heart, that struggling nations need help to grow. As a new nation, we had received help from nation-allies such as France. In the 1950s and '60s, confronting the "explosion" of Africa into new countries, we had taken steps to help them. But the promise of independence, as always, was easier than the reality. Once the new constitutions were adopted and the new flags flown, once the difficult task began of building nations behind the bright banners and manifestoes, our support fell short of what it might have been. It is not that the United States could—or should—have tried to pay for and to manage and solve the problems of Africans. Helping need not be meddling. But as we flew toward that conference in Lagos, I could see how much more we might have done to help.

At the conference, I said so. First I said that the level of American aid on behalf of that continent ought to be increased, that our aid giving ought to be reformed so that we could more readily and more usefully accommodate the planned objectives of the individual African countries. We were tending to a regional approach to aid and, although I support increased multilateral aid, I thought it was not wholly adequate to the needs of particular African states. The Africans were concerned about this.

The second basic comment I wanted to make was that I thought we would have to assume a more positive responsibility on the problems of racism and colonialism on the African continent.

With respect to South Africa, we should consider ways of making clear our disapproval of its apartheid policies. One way might be the elimination of the sugar quota that we award to South Africa. Or we might move our space tracking station from South Africa to another location. That might be minor in the sense of any impact on the South African economy, but major in the sense of indicating our convictions. We ought to look for effective steps to take with respect to American business activities in South Africa. I don't think that we ought to isolate South Africa because that would be counterproductive. But the argument against isolation should not become an excuse for tacit support of racist policies. Many of the Black African nations felt that way, too, I sensed. And I thought we ought to take serious steps with Portugal on that nation's insistence upon maintaining colonies in Africa. The Africans knew that we continued to give Portugal military assistance as a NATO ally. They knew that Portugal then traded dollars to use their own money more effectively to support military operations in the colonies. Again, I think that if we were to cut off military assistance to Portugal it might not be critical to them, but it would be an important signal to the Africans as well as an important indication to Portugal of our anti-colonialism.

The talk seemed to be well received by the African leaders there. Throughout the next three or four days, I got favorable comments. One of their leaders was generous enough to say that he thought it was one of the most forthright American statements on Africa since Robert Kennedy's.

General Gowan, who was our host, is a young man of thirty-four. He is attractive and modest. When he invited me to visit him, he wanted me above all to meet his one-year-old son—and that was the first happy event when I arrived in his office. The policy in which he takes most pride is his movement to a reconciliation with the eastern region that tried to secede as Biafra. He thinks of Abraham Lincoln's proposed policies for reconciliation after the Civil War as a historical precedent. That is a revealing insight as to the kind of man he is. He is thought of by his people as a good man, with decent instincts and humanitarian values. Whether or not he can survive the political infighting, which is bound to develop, is a question to which I have no answer. He said that he has to hold power until 1976. That is a long time to restrain the political energy that Nigeria is capable of generating. The one note of active dissatisfaction we picked up in Lagos was expressed by a number of Nigerians who said that the announcement that they would not return to civilian rule until 1976 was causing deep doubts and questions, and they expected pressures to build up on the government.

Most Americans, when we think of Africa at all, think in terms of Victoria Falls, the jungles of Kenya, the animals, and its considerable beauty. Nigeria is on the West Coast and at the time we were there it was very hot and muggy. The coastal region is flat and not particularly picturesque. Most of us think of Africa in tribal terms, but Nigeria, and especially Lagos, is developed much beyond that point. The Nigerians have acquired many of the features of our urban, affluent society, including the abrupt contrasts between wealth and abject poverty. But the people are cheerfully disposed, even though they have much to be uncheerful about, and they have considerable energy, in spite of the climate.

Sir Seretse Khama, President of Botswana, who was exiled in England for a long time before his country achieved its independence, was one of the impressive personalities at the conference. He is regarded as one of the most effective Black African leaders, moderate in his approach, yet committed to principles of independence, equality, and anti-colonialism. He is quiet, extremely intelligent, and most effective in presenting his point of view, even though he is not an orator. Sir Seretse is articulate and lucid, speaking with poise, restraint, and patience. His country is a small one, just north of and contiguous to South Africa. It is all Black. Many of its people work in South Africa under the rules of apartheid. It is almost wholly dependent economically upon South Africa. Its access to the sea and its shipping routes are through South Africa. So Khama has to be very careful of the policies he adopts to resist and fight racism and colonialism. He is in a tight squeeze, he walks a tight line, but he has maintained credibility with African leaders all over the continent. They respect him. Leaders in more powerful nations could well follow his example.

Each of the dialogue sessions was led by an African and an American discussion leader. There were a number of specific topics, but the two issues that emerged constantly were racism and colonialism. Both were caught up in United

States domestic and foreign policies. Several of the American Black delegates undertook to interpret Africa's problems as an extension of America's domestic problems of racism. They were eager for the African countries to exert an influence on the United States by such tactics as insisting on Black United States ambassadors. The Africans regarded some of these suggestions as contrary to their own interests, but there was no disagreement over the ways in which racial prejudice and discrimination had hurt African countries in their efforts to overcome the vestiges of colonialism. I had gone to the conference intellectually convinced that colonial policies were evil. I came away with a solid conviction that the United States should never again contribute to such an inhumane subjugation of people.

One of the best aspects of the conference for me was the chance to get to know Whitney Young, Jr. We had opportunities to talk at the conference sessions and at meals, including one long lunch. We went swimming twice, in the ocean and in the hotel pool, and in those days I was impressed, again and again, by his cheerful, buoyant, vigorous spirit. I had to leave the conference early and it was a terrible shock when we landed in London to learn of his death just a few hours after we left Lagos.

I had really known him for just a few days, but I shared with those who knew Whitney Young for many years the distress at his loss. He was a man who could talk to Blacks and to whites, to keep the respect of each, and to keep the lines open. Men to build those bridges are in short supply. He seemed to feel a responsibility to talk to groups who couldn't talk to each other. Certainly he believed in America, and the potential for this becoming a country of not only promise, but fulfillment, for Blacks as well as for whites. He was interested in building on what we have rather than tearing it down. And he sought communication as the essential key to that objective. The Reverend Jesse Jackson said, shortly afterward: "When God spoke in his own eternal way to Whitney on Thursday, he did so with him on his job, in his motherland, Africa—not here on romance, not here on fantasy, but here trying to hook up the roots and the fruits of an African and an Afro-American civilization. . . ."

What Jesse Jackson had said in eulogy reminded me of the difference in the way our fathers had come to the United States. Yet despite the fact of slavery and the history of other indignities heaped upon the Black man, their goals had turned out to be the same.

I must add here, in the context of world community, the history of one other journey, the distance I traveled not to a country or continent, but in thinking about one. I refer, of course, to the road I traveled in changing my convictions about the war in Vietnam.

When I wrote to President Lyndon Johnson, urging a halt to the bombing by our planes, I was not, to understate the case, a student of Asia or of U.S.-Asian relationships. Although I had majored in history and government, the emphasis was on government, *our* government, and my study of world history was not, unfortunately, nearly comprehensive enough.

To me, during much of my young life, Asia was a piece of geography. There was, of course, that period in the thirties when the Japanese aggression in China began and we became conscious of and concerned with military action activities there. I had learned to think highly of Sun Yat Sen, principally because he was identified in our eyes with democracy, which we then thought (and continued to) was the answer to everybody's ills . . . including those who didn't want a cure.

Like the rest of us, I knew something—or thought I did—about China: the Boxer Rebellion, the Open Door policy, all the standard events in the occidental view of oriental history. But these were political matters, seen from here, and they gave little insight into the people of any Asian country—who they were, what they were like, how they differed in aspirations, hopes, processes, prospects.

Then, during World War II, many Americans came to know a little more about that part of the world, but not enough so that it could be said that most of us understood the Asian peoples. There were, too, the consequences of that state of mind produced during that war, when Chiang and the Chungking Government were our allies against the Japanese. Our allies were the good guys in the white hats. Almost all other Orientals were enemies or to be ignored or undifferentiated. Thus, we constantly oversimplified, preoccupied with our own problems closer to home, not realizing yet that the whole planet was home.

We dealt in cartoon images and papier-mâché constructions of reality. How could we have known the Asians without more intimate, firsthand experience? For they were hidden peoples, colonial subjects with little or no chance at self-expression or self-government for a long time—centuries in some cases. President Roosevelt opposed the restoration of colonialism in Southeast Asia, but he did not live to implement that policy. Then Asia—as it had before—became tangled in European-American politics. Our desire to form the NATO alliance required France's participation at a time when the French were seeking to re-establish control in Southeast Asia. The barter was not explicit, but it blunted the edges of whatever hard information we might have received about the Southeast Asians while we sought, in understandable anxiety, to create a strong mutual defense system in Western Europe. Preoccupied once again, this time with the threat of communism and the cold war, we were unable to focus early on a "distant" sector such as Indochina and we could not or would not see the unrest and the forces of nationalism that were emerging. Many of us regarded the ouster of Chiang from the Chinese mainland and the triumph of Mao as a victory for the monolith of international communism, as a threat to the free world. When these events occurred, we saw them as the fall of China, not a change of government. We saw the early actions and attitudes of "Red China" in much the same light that we regarded the growing intransigence of the Soviet Union. When challenged, we moved militarily to show how important it was to call a halt to Communist incursions into South Korea. We were disturbed by the fall of the French "fortress" of Dienbienphu and the partition of Indochina. We did not pay enough attention, or bear down deeply, on the Geneva accords, on the implications of that settlement. I'm sure some of our leaders did, but I am writing now of what I saw as a very domestic citizen. Nineteen fifty-four, the year of the Geneva accords, was the year I was elected governor and my attention did not span Southeast Asia.

The fall of China had been used as an issue in the campaign of 1952. The Republicans blamed the Democrats for losing China, and, when the time came and they were newly in power, the Republicans were not about to "lose" Indochina if they could avoid it. Once again, we scribed a line in the dust, over which the Communists ought not to be allowed to pass. President Eisenhower's offer to be of economic assistance to Diem and the government that emerged in Saigon was regarded as being in the American interest. I don't think many of us knew that we were doing nothing to implement the mandate for elections set up by the Geneva accords, and that we were, in fact, blocking them. President Eisenhower later wrote that it had become fairly evident that had elections been held that Ho Chi Minh might well have been President, and we certainly did little or nothing to hasten the electoral process.

That was perhaps the last time before our entry into the war that we had an opportunity to see the situation resolved by a political settlement. The resolution might not have been one we liked, but it would have been a settlement. I think now that we, for our part, should have accepted it.

When the difficulties of the Diems began to surface, we started to suspect that we had backed the wrong horse. It was not engaging the loyalty and support of the people of South Vietnam and the guerrilla warfare was a reaction, in part, to that regime. This unstable situation required us to put in more and more economic assistance, and that seemed to require us in turn to send in military advisers. (Some of our economic assistance was in the form of hardware and, I presume, prudent economics meant trying to make sure that such military material was being used properly.)

President Kennedy was faced with a more difficult situation and, caught in the momentum, he increased the number of advisers to some sixteen thousand. This was a lot of advice —and nothing he did in peripheral ways slowed the instability, the fighting, or the violence.

There was a period in the middle 1960s when the picture we were given was of the enemy escalating his forces. There was disagreement about whether the enemy was wholly Vietcong, that is, South Vietnamese rebelling against the government, or whether it included North Vietnamese forces. All we were doing by escalating, it was said, was countering their build-up so that they could not defeat, and take over, South Vietnam. "Measured response" was the phrase used, as I recall.

In late 1965, Senator Mike Mansfield organized a round-the-world trip which had presidential approval. We went, in fact, in the presidential jet. Senator Mansfield had invited a small bipartisan group to accompany him, including Senators Aiken, Boggs, Inouye, and me. We went into thirteen countries on that visit,* to explore the possibilities of peace initiatives and to determine official attitudes toward the war.

The document which we issued, the "Mansfield Report," was one of the early shockers. Our trip had caused us to become concerned that we were involved in an open-ended conflict, one that could lead to the land war in Asia which we had always been against. At that time our troop commitment was close to 200,000 men, and I remember that the impression we got from military briefings was that conceivably the commitment of as many as a million Americans might be called for before the war was over.

We warned against that—and the warning was a surprise to many. Until that point, as I have written, most of us had more or less accepted the idea that President Johnson was on top of the situation, that he knew how to manage these things, that he was orchestrating it effectively, balancing the limited American involvement against the danger of full-scale war. We had believed that what we were doing was necessary to contain the Communist threat in Southeast Asia.

The Mansfield mission's statement was not the first public opposition by responsible leaders, but it was significant. I still accepted the President's stated objective, that he wanted simply to prevent the collapse of the South Vietnamese Gov-

---

* France, Poland, U.S.S.R., Rumania, Ceylon, Burma, Thailand, Laos, Cambodia, Vietnam, Hong Kong, Philippines, and Japan.

ernment and society, using force but not enough to trigger a nuclear war. I knew, for example, that the President had rejected the recommendation that we go into Cambodia, of going into Laos, and of other military initiatives. He was severely criticized by Republicans for doing so. There were many restraints that he imposed, while being painted as a weak leader on one side and as a warmonger on the other. Still, there was reason for concern in that some of the initial restraints were being lifted gradually in order to put more pressure on the North Vietnamese.

The issues then began to undergo further debate in the Fulbright hearings in 1966. These presented to the country the spectacle of American leaders questioning the war in the sharpest terms. And there, I think, was the beginning of the other escalation, of public resistance to the war, and toward the unhelpful division of opinion into "hawks and doves." I was disturbed by the question of whether we were diluting our ability to end the war by the barrage of criticism here at home. That concern, more than any other (except perhaps the suspicion that I didn't have all the answers to all the world's difficult questions), prompted me not to be too vocal or too critical in public. I raised my doubts in other ways. The whole question remains and may never be answered—whether our efforts might have been more effective, and whether the war could have ended sooner, had our critics been more restrained or had those of us with doubts been more vocal. That is for the historians to argue.

I am sure, as some charged, that the enemy took comfort from it all. But no matter what happened in Hanoi, we were beginning to face the moral implications of the war. Clearly, there were questions we should have considered earlier. This was not war in our terms. This was not war in our experience. It was, and we should have acknowledged the consequences, guerrilla warfare. Guerrilla war means the killing of civilians. A guerrilla war, for that matter, *invites* the use of civilians as military accomplices. In war, innocent people die; in guerrilla warfare, many innocent people die. The Vietnamese were indistinguishable to many American eyes, both because of their unfamiliar features and because of the unforgettable fact that some "civilians" were Vietcong, even as others were peaceful farmers and villagers. This had to result in the defensive or aggressive reaction of troops that meant the death of innocents as well as enemies. It was happening, we came to see, on the ground and from the air. President Johnson felt confident, based on what he had been told, that bombing techniques and technology could pinpoint military targets and not destroy civilian areas. It was efficient, but the bombing did kill non-combatants, too.

It compounded the problem when our troops encountered a civilian population, much of which had no particular national allegiance. Many Vietnamese live totally within their local environments; they understand no national loyalty as we know it. Whether or not they felt any special allegiance to "their" government in Saigon, there was an additional factor: The civilians had to live with Vietcong who either infiltrated or were welcomed into their villages at night. People caught in such a trap are concerned with personal survival. They are going to try to live with both sides, to live with everybody who threatens them. They are, in short, going to try to live.

As for the "alliance" itself, we had become involved with South Vietnam at a point when there was not, in reality, a country of South Vietnam. It was instead a place which had been divided into two zones. The people who felt oriented toward Ho Chi Minh lived in or moved north. Others, who did not elect Ho's brand of communism, moved south. The

biggest movement was from north to south, some 900,000
to a million. Ho, who had been the leader of the Nationalist
forces during World War II, had been in a position to organize a government and to make his strength felt upon the
people. In South Vietnam, there was no core of comparable
leadership. Diem was chosen, with some help from us, as the
best prospect for the formation of a government. The relationship we began, and the alliance we eventually formed,
was not with a going concern, a traditional government; instead, we undertook to help create a government and to
build a nation where none had existed before. Thus, Vietnam offered in no sense the kind of alliance we had experienced with established countries in Europe. It was an amor-
phous, loose situation at best.

Our initial effort, in the form of a letter from President
Eisenhower in 1954, offered economic assistance and guid-
ance to enable South Vietnam to build up a capability to
resist aggression. It was in the same year that Secretary of
State John Foster Dulles pushed for the formation of the
SEATO alliance, the purpose of which was to put together
quickly a military defense mechanism to contain the Communist threat along the line that had been drawn in South
Vietnam. (South Vietnam had not even been referred to as
"South Vietnam" up to that point, and a protocol to the
treaty was the first such reference to it as a country.)

To be fair, we had spent many years in building up similar
organizations—starting with NATO. The reasons for doing so
after World War II were perfectly plain. But it is conceivable
that the whole effort, this chain of defensive devices, got out
of hand, off balance. I am not at all confident that SEATO
and SENTO were viable military alliances from the beginning. SENTO includes a collection of countries in no position
to create a workable military force.

I believe the time has come to reconsider these treaties, pacts, and alliances. As Clark Clifford found in his first travels as Secretary of Defense, the very countries whose safety SEATO was meant to assure were reluctant to commit troops to the defense of South Vietnam. Militarily, they hesitated, and, politically, they found it dangerous. So even if the domino theory had been a correct forecast, many of the dominoes would not move to prevent their own fall. Perhaps dominoes do not see the game as the players do.

The network of agreements built up over the past twenty-five years needs searching re-examination. What has happened in Vietnam could happen again—and elsewhere. It would be poor international psychology to invalidate some of our agreements or to ignore them; that is not the American style. But we ought to refuse to be bound *ad infinitum* by aging treaty obligations. The conditions, the terms, under which treaties are set up, change. We honor what we have put our names to, and we should not give up the practice, or of responding to promises, pledges, and formal commitments. But the world has moved since we set out to encircle the Communist bloc with free world alliances; it has not gotten any less dangerous, perhaps, but certainly world power shifts and so do "vital interests."

Whether or not all our existing alliances will work in the future, they were sought after as a deliberate part of our national policy. Constructing them was part of the wisdom of the time—another time. We debate the morality of our continued participation in the war in Vietnam; we must also debate the morality of having signed contracts we may no longer care to live up to, or of leading other peoples to think that we will come to their aid if we will not or cannot. We should have learned from the SEATO-Vietnam experience, at least, to put limits on our obligations, to refuse to pledge ourselves to open-ended costs in lives and money and penalties on progress within the United States. The Presidents and the administrations who got us into Vietnam and expanded our engagement there were not evil or avaricious men. The more one studies the background of our involvement, the less clear-cut are the explanations of why we did what we did. Our motivation at the outset, in about 1954, when we regarded the scene in Indochina as a confrontation with international communism, made some form of aid or intervention seem essential in the interests of our own and of allied people's long-term security. I am sure that such was the overriding motivation of our leaders.

I doubt very much that many people today would believe that the American interest justifies the kind of bloody involvement that came to pass. History may change that judgment, but I am convinced that our involvement was wrong—wrong for the Vietnamese, wrong for the cause of peace in Indochina, and wrong for our country. It is the kind of mistake we should not repeat.

Another factor in those promises and pledges did come into play at one point. Our government saw the importance of maintaining the credibility of American commitments and of American military power and influence. There was the feeling that having become involved, we had to disengage creditably, without leaving collapse and chaos behind us. There was a risk that if we did, we would diminish the belief in the ability and the willingness of the United States to meet our commitments elsewhere in the world. More and more, I think, that replaced other purposes and became the dominant motivation of our national leaders and policies.

There was a final and related idea that having begun all this aid and doubtful comfort to the Vietnamese, having irrevocably changed their country and its prospects, for better and worse, we had a responsibility to see it through. We could not run out on them because we had convinced ourselves that we were wrong. This kind of thought, too, became a thread in the curious skein of American attitudes.

There is no way that I can see which will assure us of being satisfied with what finally occurs in Vietnam. We cannot be certain that Hanoi will not eventually control the whole country. We cannot know that Saigon will remain non-Communist. We cannot be sure that the fighting will not continue, perhaps for years to come. We cannot be certain that other countries will not become involved and, possibly, fall; countries like Laos and Thailand, stanch allies who have made real commitments. Cambodia, Burma . . . all of these are vulnerable and conceivably have been made more, not less, vulnerable by our unresolved, expensive involvement over these years.

Even if the domino theory turns out to be prophetic, at least in part, I do not think that we would look at the results today in the same terms of America's vital interests as when the idea was conceived. We would be concerned, to be sure, but I don't think we would regard it in world terms as apocalyptic. We have come too close to apocalypse in recent decades to see all setbacks and disappointments as the end of the world.

What is important—and what may be, and I hope will be, overtaken by events before this book appears—is to end our involvement in the war and to encourage a political settlement. That means getting all our troops out safely and obtaining the release of our prisoners of war. It means making clear to the Saigon Government that we are not committed to support a regime that is committed to continue the war.

The political settlement we would like to see would have safeguards for the people of South Vietnam. But there is no way to get an absolute guarantee for them, either. Is it not better, then, to encourage the best political settlement we can, transferring the struggle in the immediate future to the talky political meeting rooms rather than keeping it in the bloody military arena?

President Nixon said, in mid-1971, that the war was not going to be an issue in 1972, or that anybody who thought the war was going to be an issue was wrong. I would like to avoid excessive partisanship, or the creation of scapegoats, but our part in the Vietnamese war will continue to be an "issue" in our minds and in our national life for years to come.

Obviously, the President had reason to hope that the war would not become further politicized here, to the detriment of a settlement. He surely felt the pressure to end our participation and he may well have been concerned also about the postwar situation in both Vietnam and the United States— an uncertain future that may well have drastic political repercussions. Whether this pressure resulted in his withdrawing more quickly than he might like or than might be prudent, or whether it resulted in his trying to put a better face on his policy and deferring postwar problems, is still unresolved.

In any case, he has lost valuable time. It seems to me that if President Nixon had used a deadline for withdrawal a year earlier, we could have ended the war earlier and gotten a better result out of it.

The morality of our first entry into the war, and of our persisting presence, has been much argued. More than one kind of moral question is embedded in the matter. There remains the question of the morality of a big power like the United States using its power in the way we have on the other side of the globe. Putting aside all of the motivations discussed, this other question still must be considered. As it turns out, there was no military confrontation with Red China. Because I have no access to military intelligence, I do not know whether that ever was a genuine, imminent danger or whether that danger heightened at any point. But without such an antagonist, what kind of a picture do we pose for the peoples of the world when we apparently use the enormous power, man power, fire power, destructive power, money power, of the greatest technological society on the face of the earth to pound a little backward area of the world? It must seem to others that we're saying: "We'll save you if it kills you." Is this the way a world power should use its influence to improve the condition of man? I think not.

The American people have concluded that it is morally wrong for us to use this power in such a place, at such a time, at such a rate. We must be wiser and more restrained and more effective in others ways; and if we can't find those other ways then we are not great, because greatness is much more than punishing military might. Indeed, I suppose, it is something completely different from pure military power; muscle is not the same as might; force is not a synonym for strength. Not that we don't need military power in a hostile world; that isn't the point.

Consider the continents of Africa and Latin America. The affairs of some of their countries are in a mess, and I use that in a descriptive rather than an accusatory way, for reasons that are connected at least as much with the intervention of outside powers as with their own internal difficulties. These several societies have not yet found all the ways to build and to develop which will serve the needs of the masses of their people. They are struggling through the morass of the political institutions and conditions and policies and strains created because of the failure to accommodate the immense wealth of the few to the tragic poverty of the many. There is no way for any power, the Soviet Union or us or Red China, to merely move into these continents and in a massive application of might to straighten out their problems. There is no single way to do it.

Does that mean, therefore, that there is nothing we should or can do? Of course not. But our aid has to take forms other than merely military. It must involve the use of material things, like money, and of humane economic policies, institutions, and instruments. It has to be done through governments which hopefully come to be increasingly responsive, or can be made increasingly responsive, to their people's needs, without our intervention. It will take the kind of leadership and example and assistance that will help these countries to generate more viable societies out of their own resources, out of their own people, out of their own leaders. This is a difficult way to use power, and in some respects restrained power is tougher than power expended in crude and violent terms. It requires a softness of heart and a toughness of mind.

The consequences for our people are as serious as those for others. If our young and our future generations grow up in this country no longer believing that we are good people, because we do not seem to act like good people, they will less and less behave like good people. A healthy self-image works for a man or a nation. We are beginning to doubt whether we are "good guys" or whether we are capable of acting like good guys. We are beginning to doubt whether, if we are good, there are enough of us to make things work.

I must say that I think there is still, on the whole, a deep desire on the part of other peoples, especially those in undeveloped countries, to see America become what they always thought America has been. They are puzzled and resentful, I think, that the nation of the Marshall Plan and CARE packages, of generosity and courage, has fallen short of what they thought we were. The South Vietnamese adventure disturbs them most. Yes, there is still much for us to build on, if we don't delay too long.

Such sentiments do not give us the means or programs or the policies to fit particular and difficult situations. Our objectives and goals ought to be clearly stated, and ought to be made credible by specific actions. To the extent that we can do so, to the extent that the picture of what we now plan to do is clear, the task becomes somewhat easier. We must re-articulate and, if necessary, redefine our goals. We have to perform specific acts to reassure people that we really intend to be helpful—but to be of help in wiser ways than the very recent past. We have to reassure people that we are committed to humanistic values and not simply to the support of establishments, repressive and otherwise. We have to be candid in saying that we cannot hope or expect to manage their situations for them, that we would like to *help* them, rather than run them or run their lives for them. We must look for ways to show that our instincts are increasingly generous and our actions, we hope, increasingly wiser.

A persistent difficulty is to be influential in countries which exist under governments which do not intend to serve their people's best interest. To try to bypass governments is to invite the kind of intervention which leads to Vietnams. The levers of power are not always visible, but if we find the right lever, if we move carefully and sensitively, and have patience over time, gradually we can change the nature of our influence and its impact.

We have the problem, also, of educating our own people on the proper roles for the United States once we've decided what our roles ought to be. And that is not easy, either. To so many citizens foreign aid is like exported welfare; it signifies taking money out of our pockets and programs and shipping it to ungrateful people elsewhere. More liberal trade policies are seen as shifting jobs from undeveloped areas of this country to undeveloped areas in other countries.

One answer, naturally, is to develop improved institutions for multinational policies. We don't really have one in the field of trade. We have one objective of liberalized trade, but not one which considers the adjustment problems which this entails for the internal economies of others. Each trading nation shapes its own protectionist rules in terms of its own interest, while pressing other countries to be more liberal in tearing down their trade barriers. The economic adjustment problem is a very serious one, but we have to find answers to it. If we do not, then what we will have is growing economic isolationism within the developed countries and a growing resentment within the undeveloped ones. To pretend that there is no price to be paid for liberal trade in industrialized countries is simply to overlook a reality.

And so, as we extricate ourselves from Vietnam, we cannot withdraw from the world or stop learning the lessons of leadership.

We no longer have the "simple" answers of cold war logic. No man, no nation should seek to divide the world up into dominated territories or spheres of influence. For one of the hard lessons I have learned is that the world is full of differences but that it does not divide.

Conclusion

As I CONCLUDE this book, the crisis in confidence that plagued Lyndon Johnson in the last years of his presidency is still with us. Americans are uncertain about themselves, their country, and their government. For those of us who beat our way up and out of the Depression and through World War II, the erosion of public confidence is hard to believe, but it has happened and we must deal with it. The credibility of a government and its leaders is not terribly important in an authoritarian society, but credibility is essential to the survival of a democracy.

Too many Americans do not believe any more that the White House or the Congress or the State House or the Legislature truly relates to their day-to-day needs. Indeed, they believe increasingly in the reverse. They suspect that government is more concerned with public relations than with relating to the public, that government is insensitive to the average citizen, and that government covers up, conceals, or lies about its intentions and its actions.

I would not argue that we should try to reverse a healthy American skepticism about politics and politicians, but we cannot survive a continued and steady deterioration of conviction about the elemental honesty and good heart of most public officials. We cannot redeem the reputations of all elected officials, but we should give urgent attention to the office of President of the United States. Both the person and the office of the President have a special place in the minds and the spirit of most Americans. They don't have to agree with him, but they do want to believe in him. They want to believe that he represents, however fallibly, the best in American ideals, objectives, and dreams. The presidency no longer enjoys that respect, and I refer not to a man, but to the office.

The most immediate cause of this lack of respect has been the war in Indochina and the general feeling that American citizens were denied the truth about our involvement there. That feeling has been compounded by our incursion in Cambodia, our peculiar behavior toward India and Pakistan during the Bangladesh crisis, and the Haynsworth, Carswell, and Justice Department-ITT cases—all of which involve decisions made by the President or his closest advisers. And when apparent duplicity in the conduct of foreign and domestic policy has been compounded by failures to solve problems that require government action, we should not be surprised when public suspicion mounts. Americans in every section of the country are frustrated by the number and complexity of our problems, and by our failure to make a dent in the incidence of crime, the backlog in educational needs, persistent unemployment, inflation and housing shortages, unfair taxes, pollution, inadequate health care, poverty, and racial tensions. They wonder if there is any real way to make a change.

In such a climate the way of the demagogue is easy. He can play on fears, exacerbate frictions, exaggerate difficulties and differences. There is in the successful demagogue a touch of genius, but such candidates make effective speeches and poor Presidents. The demagogic approach is unworthy of our democratic society and it should be attacked whenever it appears, but there is no reason why an honorable candidate cannot speak to the decent, understandable fears of the voters. For example, many Americans—Black and white—feel that busing is an unsatisfactory permanent, long-term solution to equal opportunities in quality education. To ignore their genuine concerns is to deny their right to be heard and to influence public policy. But recognizing their concerns does not require that we ignore the use of busing in some cases as a step toward improved and integrated educational opportunities for all our children. Put in its proper context, busing can be seen as a limited series of short rides rather than a long journey down a highway with no end. And the answer to the problem of equal opportunity in education will be found not simply in speaking the truth about segregated education and housing and jobs, but in building a coalition for change among Blacks and whites.

That same coalition will be needed to overcome discrimination in housing and unemployment, and neither of these problems can be resolved without a healthy, growing economy. So long as the economy is stagnant, and so long as we have a national economic policy geared to using unemployment as a deliberate tool in the control of inflation, tensions will remain between whites and Blacks at the lower end of the economic scale. As long as these tensions exist, demagogues can have a field day, exploiting the fears of men and women struggling to make ends meet, to find decent housing, and to give their children a better chance.

Our economic troubles are particularly difficult because we had assumed that we had found the way to permanent prosperity, and all the rosy rhetoric of the Nixon administration has only succeeded in highlighting the harsh reality of unemployment for the young and the old, Blacks and whites, men and women, rural dwellers and ghetto residents, laborers and professionals. Those of us who are over forty can never forget the impact of the Depression and what a destructive force unemployment was in this country. We hoped we would not see it again, but we are.

I was reminded of the horrors of the Depression not long ago when I watched some interviews with people in Seattle, Washington, who had been laid off. They were facing circumstances that are all too familiar to lower income groups in our society, but because those circumstances were so unexpected there was an added dimension of pain. These were college-trained people without jobs. They were engineers and managers who had been employed in the glamour industry of our country, aerospace. They were well dressed and comfortably housed, but they found themselves no longer needed. Some were doing janitorial work and were glad to get it, considering themselves fortunate by comparison with others who could not find such employment.

In a way, there was a grim educational process taking place. People of the "white middle class" were beginning to identify, some for the first time, with those of other colors and classes who are chronically poor and unemployed. They never dreamed it could happen to them. It is not only the loss of income; it is the destructive loss of purpose. What do you do with your spare time, when all your time is "spare"? How do you spend the day? How do you explain to your children when they need something and you can no longer provide it? What do you do about your home when the mortgage payments can't be met? What do you do about the car, and when that is gone, how do you get about? And how do you maintain any semblance of self-respect and family life and hope for the future?

It is this side of unemployment that too often is overlooked when calculated unemployment is used as part of a policy to deal with inflation.

There are reasons for inflation and for unemployment, but not very good ones for sustaining them. As I have said, in my opinion the President failed to act soon enough on controls and he has even opposed programs to stimulate employment. He vetoed public works bills enacted by Congress to create jobs; he vetoed a public service employment legislation when enacted by the Congress to deal with unemployment; he fought amendments to tax laws which would have stimulated consumer buying. And tax "relief" has been, for most people, anything but.

The underlying resentment against unfair taxes has led to a flurry of taxpayer revolts in many sections of the country, almost all being directed against the property tax, which may well be the most unpopular tax in the United States today. The property owner is asked to carry burdens in supporting public services that property taxes were not originally designed to carry. The property tax, initially, was to help pay for public services related in one way or another to the use of the property street lighting, cleaning, fire protection, and police protection. The property owner and taxpayer now must support other social services, and the fact that a citizen owns property does not necessarily reflect his ability to pay. Senior citizens, for example, have invested much of their economic life's rewards in their homes. Yet they must continue to pay property taxes to support public services which, as older people, they require. And in too many instances the property taxes for senior citizens exceed the payments they made to buy their homes in the first place.

The situation is equally distressing for the poor. (And some of our older citizens qualify as both.) Either through rental payments or mortgaged money, the poor are required to bear the burden of property taxes that exceed their ability to pay. The city of Newark provides a dramatic illustration. A home there with a market value of $10,000 today is subject to over $900 a year in property taxes. That means that the total value of the house is consumed by taxes in eleven years. Who, then, wants to own property in Newark (other than slum lords)? And that creates one of our newer urban problems: People are walking away from property. The federal government could help to lift the property tax burden by picking up more of the costs of education. Federal assumption of more welfare costs would be another way of relieving the burden on state and local budgets, as well as private ones. An enlightened form of revenue sharing, which would use federal funds for budgetary support at the state and local levels, is another way of relieving the burden.

Raising public revenues through a more equitable tax system will not, in and of itself, solve all our problems. We have to decide how best to spend those resources we allocate for public needs. How much should we spend on schools, health, welfare, housing, jobs, pollution control, transportation, and conservation? How much should we spend on war and defense?

In spite of the reaction against the war in Vietnam, there is still a tendency to put national military security first in our budget planning. In spite of the lessons of the arms race, we tend to overbuy military weapons, looking for the perfect defense against our prospective enemies. We should have learned by now that piling up arms does not buy security. Only when we had a nuclear monopoly did we feel clearly "superior," and that did not last for long. As the nuclear arms race proceeded, the more arms we stock-piled, the less secure we felt. The Soviet Union reacted to our growing nuclear stock pile by piling up their own, and the escalation brought insecurity for both sides.

How do we get this turned around? First, we must identify our real security needs in terms of a suitable defense and agree upon what it will take to meet our real needs, not exaggerated claims. Second, we must engage in negotiations with other nuclear powers in the mutual interest of stabilizing the arms race and reducing costs. Arms are the conventional route to security, but arms alone do not do the job. That does not mean that we dispense with them. It means that we insist on becoming more reasonable and rational about what is needed for defense and what resources can be released for other needs and goals.

That is the sort of question that leads to a more fundamental problem, the issue of what America's role should be in the world of the immediate future. Since World War II, we have been the most powerful nation in terms of arms. Indeed, we have been more powerful than any nation in the world's history, and we have tended to use our military power more visibly than any of the other great nations. In Vietnam, we learned at great cost what damage we could do to ourselves and others by the mistaken use of military power. Apart from whether or not it was right to use that power in every case, we should ask ourselves what really strengthens our influence in the world. Economic and military power do have an impact, but they are not the most effective forces on behalf of a free society.

What gives America its greatest influence, I think, is our actions at those times when we most closely reflect our national ideals. Our influence and true power were greatest when America was a place of hope for her own people and for others abroad. Our example was best set not by attempts to impose our system on others, but by offering the model of people living in reasonable harmony, which was reassuring to others who found in it hope and a chance for their own improvement. It was hope that brought forty million immigrants on a journey to this country, and hope that animated the nation itself. People came here and found reason for hope, and people lived in their own lands and found heart in our hope.

I do not believe this view of history is naive. The basic forces that create history—and that will have an even greater impact in the years ahead—are the elemental needs and emotions of hunger, hatred, love, fear, and frustration. These are the forces that move the vast majority of people on this planet. It will not be the sophisticated considerations, power diplomacy, chess games, or cold-war relationships that determine people's attitudes about war and peace or drive them toward either. The situations in northern Ireland, in Southeast Asia, and in Bangladesh arose out of the fact that people found themselves living in circumstances they could no longer endure. Human beings can endure a great deal, but not without hope. Sooner or later we must come to grips with these truths and understand that we cannot contain or control such forces by the force of America's nuclear arms.

Because I believe so deeply in the obligation of a democratic government to be responsive and responsible to the needs of its own citizens and the needs of our fellow residents on this planet, I hazard a campaign in which caring and truth—not just the war, the economy, public versus private interests, and the environment—are major issues. It is only through caring about each other and telling the truth about ourselves and about each other that we can begin to regain the confidence that is essential if we are to overcome those problems and shortcomings that make us unsure about what we might be and less than what we could be.

As I have tried to show in this ruminative book, I have no magic answers to those issues, but I do want to work toward restoring, win or lose, something that John Kennedy offered us, which was a sense of hope; what President Eisenhower offered, which was a sense of innate decency; what President Truman offered, which was a sense of crisp decision; what President Franklin Roosevelt offered, which was a sense of recovery and destiny.

One of the basic weaknesses in our country, today, is the fear that we have no destiny, the fear that we are not going any place, the fear that the journey toward the promise of the Declaration of Independence and the Constitution may have ended. We have a secret dread that we are sliding backward, that we have lost our possibilities as well as many of our principles and good qualities. We are concerned that the American Dream may be over, even before it had fairly begun. We approach a two hundredth birthday which, in the life span of nations, may be adulthood, but should not signal senility. It is not so long since we demonstrated our capacity to overcome the Depression and to defeat our enemies in World War II, but we have an impression today of merely coping. At best, the present Administration gives off a faint order of competence, managerial skills, and middling abilities. There is no genius, no spark, little humor, and less glory.

Our country need not be this way. The vision that moved

the founding fathers and the millions of immigrants can be rekindled. But it can only be brought to life by leaders who will not stoop to play one group against another, who will not sacrifice the public interest for the private gain of a few, and who have enough faith and confidence in the American people to challenge them with new journeys that lead not to unconquered lands and untapped physical resources, but to the achievement of "life, liberty, and the pursuit of happiness" in a finite planet where working together can make freedom and equality a reality.